The Emergence of
North Carolina's
Revolutionary State Government

For
John T. Horton

The Emergence of North Carolina's Revolutionary State Government

By
Robert L. Ganyard

Raleigh 1978

96165

CONTENTS

PREFACE

In the following pages I have sought to relate the evolution of government in North Carolina to the developing events of the American Revolution. After a discussion of the structure and problems of government under the crown, the narrative concentrates on the emergence and activities of the revolutionary congresses, committees, and councils that seized control of the colony between 1774 and 1776, thereby displacing legitimate authorities at all levels, and concludes with a discussion and analysis of the new state constitution of 1776 and the implementation of government under it. The first chapter is based to a considerable extent upon secondary accounts; the remaining chapters are based largely on primary materials.

In producing this study I have drawn largely upon my Duke University doctoral dissertation, "North Carolina during the American Revolution: The First Phase, 1774-1777," which was written under the able direction of Robert H. Woody. I am indebted to him for his guidance at that time and his friendship since. Research for that work, and consequently for this, was pursued at many libraries and depositories, including the Duke University Library and Manuscript Collection, Durham, the North Carolina Division of Archives and History, Raleigh, the Southern Historical Collection, Chapel Hill, the Rice University Library, Houston, and the Library of Congress. More recently I have utilized the facilities of the Lockwood Library, State University of New York at Buffalo. I am indebted to the staffs of all these institutions for their help and courtesy.

My debt to John T. Horton, to whom this study is dedicated, goes back many years to my undergraduate days at the University of Buffalo. His inspired teaching sparked in me and countless others a love for historical study. Since that time he has been a most amiable colleague, a wise counselor, and a fast friend. To my colleagues Selig Adler and Clifton K. Yearley I am beholden for reading portions of the manuscript and for extending encouragement in many ways over the years, and I am grateful to Suzanne Feltes for her expert job of typing. I am, of course, entirely responsible for any errors of fact or interpretation.

Lockport, New York   Robert L. Ganyard
July, 1977

Map of North Carolina, 1796, by Samuel Lewis, from the Map Collection, North Carolina State Archives.

I

The Colony and Its Government under the Crown

The royal period of North Carolina history, 1729-1776, was an era of vibrant growth and expansion. In the former year it was probably the most sparsely populated of all the English mainland colonies with only thirty to thirty-five thousand people, nearly all of them of English stock and residing in nine tidewater counties clustered around Albemarle and Pamlico sounds. During the next forty-five years the population increased tenfold, making North Carolina the fourth most populous of England's mainland colonies. The number of counties increased to thirty-five, and settlement expanded westward across the piedmont to the foothills of the Great Smokies and beyond.[1] While some of the population growth was due to natural increase, most resulted from the immigration of new settlers of diverse origins, giving to the colony a mixed population with respect to both national stocks and religion. Into the lower Cape Fear River valley in the late 1720s and the 1730s came settlers from South Carolina and the Albemarle region to establish the towns of Brunswick and Wilmington and take up lands around them. About 3,000 people lived in the area by 1740. Contemporaneously, Highland Scots, direct from Scotland, began to pass through and take up settlement on the upper Cape Fear. Arriving in small groups at first, after 1745 they came in such large numbers that by the outbreak of the Revolutionary War there were probably over 20,000 in the colony. During the same period thousands of Germans and Scotch-Irish migrated into the North Carolina backcountry, most of them coming from Pennsylvania by way of the Valley of Virginia, while many other settlers moved westward into the piedmont from the Albemarle area and southward into the north-central region from Virginia. In consequence, by the outbreak of the Revolution over half of the colony's population resided in its seven or eight westernmost counties.[2]

The various origins of North Carolina's people helped make for great religious diversity in the colony. While the Anglican church was established, it was organizationally weak. Though it claimed many adherents, the new immigrants—many of them non-English—who swelled the colony at mid-century included large numbers of dissent-

1

ers who came to equal if not outnumber the Anglicans. The Baptists and Presbyterians were the two largest dissenter sects, the latter growing with the increasing immigration of Scots. North Carolina Baptists aggregated about 40,000 by the 1770s as did the Presbyterians who settled mainly in the upper Cape Fear region and the backcountry. There were also many Quakers in the colony, and the German migration brought into the backcountry a combined Lutheran and Reformed population of nearly 20,000 plus a few hundred Moravians. Of the Quakers, there were perhaps 5,000 living principally in the old counties of the northeast. Doubtless many other people in the colony claimed no religion at all.[3]

The vast majority of North Carolina's people were farmers, and by far the greater number of these small farmers. While many produced only enough to meet their own needs, many others produced commodities for export. Provisions—corn, peas, beans, wheat, flour, livestock, beef, and pork—were important export items, along with lumber, tobacco, and naval stores, the last item ranking first in value among the colony's exports in the late colonial period. Thus, while North Carolina was not a major commercial center, its export trade was substantial, and it surpassed several other colonies commercially. Massachusetts, Pennsylvania, and Virginia far outstripped North Carolina as commercial centers, and it was outranked also by New York, Maryland, and South Carolina, but the shipping departing from its ports was greater in volume than that sailing from New Hampshire, Rhode Island, Connecticut, New Jersey, or Georgia. In 1770 over 23,000 tons of goods left North Carolina ports, and the total annual value of goods exported from its ports in the years just prior to the Revolution approximated £100,000, while an additional £100,000 in goods passed through the ports of Virginia and South Carolina. Many of North Carolina's rivers, flowing from northwest to southeast, constituted barriers to the movement of goods from east to west. Moreover, east-west roads were poor, overland transport was slow and expensive, and markets comparable to those in South Carolina and Virginia did not exist on the North Carolina coast. Consequently, much of the trade of the southern counties of the piedmont went down the Yadkin, the Catawba, and other rivers into South Carolina, most of it destined for Charleston, while much of that of the northern piedmont and the Albemarle region went to Virginia ports.

Nevertheless, commercial activity was an important and growing feature of North Carolina society, and a small but influential merchant class arose in the colony, especially after mid-century. There were a number of prominent merchants in the Cape Fear region, most of them located at Wilmington, on the coast, and at

Cross Creek, at the head of navigation. At New Bern, the colonial capital, located at the point where the Neuse River flows into Pamlico Sound, there were also mercantile houses, as there were at Edenton and Halifax in the Albemarle Sound region. There were also merchants at Tarborough and Bath, located farther inland. In the piedmont and backcountry regions mercantile establishments were fewer and their operations smaller, and in many cases they were owned by companies in the Cape Fear or Albemarle areas, Virginia, or Great Britain.[4]

Most of the important merchants resided in the principal coastal towns. Along with the substantial planters of the tidewater area they constituted the elite of North Carolina's rather stratified society, which was composed of four main classes: gentry, small farmers and artisans, indentured servants and poor whites, and Negroes. Besides planters and merchants, the gentry included public officials, the clergy of the established church, and the leading lawyers and doctors. Constituting less than 5 percent of the total population, this class was composed in the main of planters of moderate wealth who owned fewer than twenty slaves and less than 500 acres of land. There were some who owned as many as fifty slaves and several thousand acres of land, however, and a very few who possessed great wealth, like Thomas Pollock, who owned some 40,000 acres and nearly 100 slaves, and Roger Moore, who owned more than 200 slaves. The second class in the social order, composed of small farmers and artisans, but overwhelmingly of the former, contained the vast majority of the colony's people. In most cases the small farmer engaged in subsistence farming, had no servants or slaves, and possessed no more than fifty acres of land. It was the unusual farmer who owned as many as two or three hundred acres and a few servants or slaves. The indentured servant class was small by the eve of the Revolution. Gradually, white servitude had been replaced by Negro slavery as the royal period advanced. Indeed, the slave population grew tremendously during these years. There were only about 900 Negroes in the province in 1712; in 1775 there were an estimated 65,000, of whom about 50,000 lived east of the fall line, where most of the plantations were located.[5] In addition there were roughly 5,000 free blacks in North Carolina by 1790, though their lives, work, and status were severely circumscribed by white society.

Though the gentry composed by far the smallest social class, its members dominated government and politics in North Carolina on both the provincial and county levels. In theory, the royal governor held the preponderance of power, but increasingly during the royal period the representative assembly, which was largely composed of and controlled by the gentry, gained strength at the expense of the governor, so that by the eve of the Revolution it had become the dominant branch of government. As Governor Arthur Dobbs complained to the Board of Trade in 1760, the commons house "think themselves entitled to all the Privileges a British House of Commons and therefore ought not to submit to His Majesty's honble. Privy Council . . . or . . . Governor and Council here whose person they would usurp and place all in a Junto of an Assembly here."[6] This shift in power from the executive to the lower house of the legislature helped set the stage for North Carolina's role in the Revolution.

The structure of royal government in North Carolina was typical of that in the other royal colonies. In addition to the governor, who received his appointment from the crown and held office during the king's pleasure, and the elective commons house of the legislature, there was a royal council, also appointed by the crown, which functioned both as the principal body of advisers to the governor and as the upper house of the legislature. The government also included a rather elaborate court structure and a fairly complex fiscal system.

Despite the dominant position of the North Carolina lower house by the 1760s, the royal governor still had extensive power. He was, of course, the chief executive officer and the principal representative of the crown in the province, and as such he was duty bound to carry out the will of the crown and obliged to act in accordance with his commission and royal instructions. It was in this connection that he most frequently came into conflict with the lower house, for the interests of the colonials were often contrary to those of the crown. The governor thus filled a difficult position, for if his administration was to be effective he had to carry out his royal orders and at the same time get along with the elective legislature—tasks that were often incompatible.

The governor's powers included not only those of an executive sort, but certain legislative and judicial powers as well. Some powers he could exercise only with the advice and consent of his council; others he could exercise independently. His executive powers included the right, with the advice and consent of his council, to grant lands and appoint most public officials, including sheriffs (ordinarily from nominees submitted by the county courts), justices of the peace, and the higher ranking militia officers. He supervised the distribution and expenditure of all money issued by the assembly and oversaw all fairs, marts, markets, ports, and harbors. He was charged with the execution and enforcement of the acts of trade, and he was chief military officer of the colony. In that capacity he could proclaim martial law during periods of invasion or at other times when English law permitted and could employ the militia to put down riots or insurrections.

The legislative powers of the governor included the right to call, prorogue, or dissolve the assembly, actions he ordinarily took in consultation with his council. He could initiate bills in the legislature, though he rarely exercised that right, and he could veto all laws passed by the legislature. Laws approved by the governor had to be sent to England within three months after passage for crown approval. The governor's judicial powers included the authority to erect, with the advice and consent of the council, such courts of law and equity as he considered necessary. He appointed all judges except the chief justice of the province, who was appointed by the crown; he could pardon persons convicted of all crimes except treason and willful murder; and he could remit fines and forfeitures.

The commons house of the assembly, the dominant branch of government, claimed some of its powers by charter right; others it claimed on the basis of tradition—that is, that similar powers had been exercised by the assemblies of the proprietary period; others it had been granted in the commissions and instructions to the governors; still others it claimed on the ground that Parliament exercised similar power. It had the right to initiate bills, and in practice it initiated nearly all bills, for though the governor and council enjoyed this right, they seldom exercised it. No bill could become law without the assent of the lower house, and it enjoyed the exclusive right to initiate and amend money bills. The lower house also insisted that it had exclusive control over the appointment of the public treasurers.[7] By virtue of this control over the purse, the lower house not infrequently forced the governor to accede to its demands, and thus it exercised very substantial influence over him and his conduct of affairs. Although the governor and council could reject any bill passed by the lower house, they, in turn, could pass no bill into law without the latter's assent. In consequence, the lower house had the power to force "the governor and council to allow it to have and to exercise a good many general and special privileges, to which it was not intitled by written law."[8] Sometimes it even forced the governor and council to assent to bills that were contrary to royal instructions. The lower house also had an important voice in regulating the territorial system (that is, the administration of crown lands), and the governor was dependent upon the lower house for money, supplies, and troops in times of military crisis. In the area of judicial affairs, the lower house passed resolutions respecting the proper administration of justice,

5

selected, with the council, the lists of jurymen for the counties, sometimes exerted pressure on the governor to grant pardons, and participated in the passing of acts for the creation of courts.[9]

The lower house was a popularly elected body, but in a society based on deference to wealth, status, and family the candidates and representatives normally came from the gentry class. In addition, the right to vote for members of the lower house became increasingly restrictive. Prior to 1743 males twenty-one years old who had lived in their precincts for one year and had paid taxes for the preceding year could vote, but after that date only freeholders who owned at least fifty acres of land had the franchise. No matter how extensive the suffrage, however, the manner in which assembly elections were conducted made for a very unrepresentative system that lent itself admirably to corruption and exploitation by local leaders. From 1715 to 1743 voters had five votes in each election; they wrote the names of their five choices for the county's delegates on a ballot and signed it. From 1743 to 1760 the system remained the same except that the voter no longer signed his ballot, but instead enrolled his name in an open book watched over by the sheriff. In 1760 the system was changed in such a way as to increase opportunities for coercion and fraud. Thereafter, the voter cast his ballot vocally. His votes were recorded, and the candidates were permitted to inspect the poll at any time. Elections were held at the county courthouses, directly under the surveillance of the county "courthouse rings," which controlled local politics in the colony. Under such a system many voters could be coerced into casting their ballots for the candidates of the local "ring." Thus, control of the lower house was perpetuated in the hands of the most substantial men in the counties, and that house was "representative only in the sense that it was representative of the dominant class of local officials."[10]

Unrepresentative of the poorer classes, the lower house was also characterized by great inequality of representation with respect to the counties and in the late royal period with respect to population distribution as well. Throughout the colonial period the counties of the Albemarle Sound region enjoyed much stronger representation than did the other counties of the colony—so much so that that region dominated the lower house until the middle of the century and exercised an inordinate influence over its proceedings during the remainder of the royal period. On the basis of precedents established in the proprietary period, Chowan, Currituck, Pasquotank, Perquimans, and Tyrrell each sent five members to the legislature, and Bertie, three, while the remaining counties sent only two members each.

This extremely unfair situation led to bitter controversy between the Albemarle counties and the increasingly populous central and Cape Fear counties between 1746 and 1754. In the former year Governor Gabriel Johnston, who had extensive interests in the Cape Fear region, plotted to secure a more favorable quitrent law, a new representation act, and the establishment of a permanent colonial capital at New Bern by calling an assembly to meet at Wilmington in the hope that the distance would keep the Albemarle delegates, who opposed these measures, at home. His plan succeeded, and a rump assembly composed of fifteen southern delegates claimed to constitute a quorum and passed acts making New Bern the permanent capital and reducing the representation of the Albemarle counties to two members each.

The Albemarle counties protested vigorously against the "illegality" of the rump assembly to Johnston and to the crown, and in the elections of 1747 they each again returned their usual number of delegates, but the assembly refused to seat them and declared the elections in these counties null and void. Unfortunately, the crown made no decision in the matter for seven years. Meanwhile, Johnston called no new elections, the rump assembly sat from time to time, and the Albemarle counties remained completely unrepresented. Finally, in April, 1754, the crown disallowed the two laws passed by the rump assembly in 1746 but upheld the legality of the assembly itself. Again in 1754, therefore, the Albemarle counties returned five members each (except Bertie, which returned three), and they continued to do so for the remainder of the royal period. This put an end to the "representation controversy," and the Albemarle and Cape Fear counties quickly patched up their differences.[11] The population increase in the backcountry had by this time begun to threaten eastern control of the legislature "and this tended to promote an alliance of the various Tidewater interests against the growing power of the West."[12] Thus, in the late royal period, the assembly of North Carolina was a powerful body, extremely jealous of its rights— whether based on royal writ, tradition, or usurpation. Dominated by the eastern counties, despite the fact that the new west was far more populous, the assembly reflected the interests of the well-to-do, most of whom resided in the east.

The council in North Carolina was an influential body composed of from seven to twelve members chosen, normally, from among the wealthiest men in the colony. Members were appointed by the crown, usually from nominees submitted by the governor. They could be removed from office only by the crown, though the governor could suspend them for misconduct or failure to carry out their responsibilities pending a final determination of their status by the crown. The powers of the council were specified in the commissions and instructions of the governors and were both executive and legislative in nature. The governor usually acted on the advice of his council, and in some matters it was mandatory that he seek its advice and consent. In its executive capacity the council exercised substantial power in the management of the territorial system and in the general administration of the colony. It participated with the governor in the issuance of warrants and land grants and in administering the collection of quitrents. It shared in the appointment of justices and sheriffs and issued letters of patent to crown appointees in the colony, such as the chief justice and the attorney general. It heard complaints against public officials and made recommendations to the governor as to whether they should be retained in office, suspended, or dismissed. It recommended to the governor persons to fill vacancies, summoned the treasurers to exhibit their accounts, and issued orders to the sheriffs regarding tax collections. It could also appoint a panel to sit with a committee of the lower house for the purpose of auditing public accounts.

In its legislative capacity the council sat as the upper house of the legislature and its assent, along with that of the governor, was necessary before any bill could become law. It could initiate bills, except money bills, but it rarely did so. All bills had to pass three readings in each house before being submitted to the governor for his signature, and each house could amend the bills of the other, with the exception that the council could not amend money bills. The council also advised the governor regarding the calling, proroguing, or dissolving of the legislature, and he usually acted on its advice.[13]

The judicial system in North Carolina consisted of a variety of courts and officials, some serving the colony as a whole, others the individual counties. Included were courts of admiralty, chancery, superior pleas and grand sessions (also called the general, or supreme, court), oyer and terminer, inferior pleas and quarter sessions, and magistrates courts. The admiralty court, which heard maritime cases, was completely independent of the provincial government and directly under the control of the admiralty board in England, which appointed the judge and the other court officials. The court of chancery, composed of the governor and at least five councillors, dealt primarily with cases of relief against the crown, but it seldom sat. The general, or supreme, court had both original and appellate jurisdiction and could hear all pleas of the crown (including cases of treason, felony, and other crimes against the peace) as well as suits in common pleas. It was headed by the chief justice, who was appointed by the crown. Associated with him was another important crown official, the attorney general. In theory these officials were independent of the governor and legislature, but in fact they became increasingly subject to legislative influence as the lower house gradually extended authority over the developing court system in the eighteenth century.

One way in which legislative influence was extended over the court system involved the appointment of associate judges to the supreme court. From 1729 to 1746 the chief justice was assisted only by justices of the peace, who had no independent authority whatever. Only the chief justice could hold supreme sessions. A new court law of the latter year, however, provided for the appointment by the governor of three associate justices, who could hold court in the absence of the chief justice and hear and determine cases. This law also made New Bern the seat of the supreme court instead of Edenton, where it had sat previously, and provided that at least two sessions of the court be held there annually. It also divided the colony into four judicial districts, including the New Bern district, and stipulated that the chief justice must ride out on circuit each year to each of the other districts, which came to be called after the town in which court was held: Edenton, Wilmington, and Halifax.[14] By a new law of 1760 the legislature sought to exert a measure of control over the appointment and tenure of the associate judges by clauses defining their qualifications and term of office. The crown disallowed this act, but in 1762 the legislature passed a new law further broadening its authority over the judicial system, which the crown allowed to stand. Taking cognizance of the rapid development of the west, the law created a fifth judicial district with its center at Salisbury. To this district, which included nearly as much territory as the other four combined, the law assigned a special judge, to be appointed by the governor, who had full power to hold supreme sessions even though the chief justice was absent. The law also imposed limits upon the power of the attorney general, regulated the frequency and duration of sessions and the manner of initiating suits and summoning witnesses, and prescribed who could bear testimony.

In 1767 the legislature established a sixth judicial district with its center at Hillsborough and provided for the appointment therein of two associate judges. They were given powers similar to those granted to the judge of the Salisbury district. Six years later the legislature passed a new act by which it sought further to control the judicial system. The act contained two clauses that the crown found objectionable: one provided for the legal attachment of the North Carolina property of defaulting debtors living outside the colony; the other sought to decrease the authority of the superior courts by increasing that of the inferior courts, which were more directly under the legislature's influence. This act precipitated a serious court controversy that lasted throughout the remainder of the colonial period and was an important issue in the developing revolutionary crisis of 1774-1775.

The court of oyer and terminer was a criminal court composed of the chief justice, at least two assistant or associate judges, members of the council, and certain other important officials. Until 1746 this court remained largely free from legislative regulation, but by the court act of that year the assembly extended a measure of control over it. The act defined the jurisdiction of the court, giving it the authority to hear cases of treason, felony, and misdemeanor. It also provided that the supreme court on circuit could function as a court of oyer and terminer, though only if the governor issued a special commission to that effect. In successive court acts passed during the next three decades provision was made for these special criminal sessions, and the governor, in consequence, made no attempt to erect such courts independently, though he had exercised that power prior to 1746. The governor's acquiescence in the exercise of authority by the assembly in the establishment of these criminal courts resulted in the assembly taking the position, by 1773, that he could not independently issue commissions for such courts without its authority. This position of the assembly created another bitter issue in the court controversy of that year.

The inferior, or county courts (courts of pleas and quarter sessions), were established in North Carolina under the proprietors and continued to function after the colony became royal in much the same manner as they had in the earlier period. Each county court was composed of several justices of the peace who were appointed by the governor and sat together several times a year to hear civil cases involving sums of less than £50. In 1746 this system, like the superior court system, was brought more directly under legislative control by the court law of that year. It provided that at least four sessions be held by each county court annually, at each of which at least three justices must preside. They could hear virtually all cases under the common law involving sums of more than 40 shillings and less than £20 as well as petty larcenies, assaults, batteries, trespasses, breaches of the peace, and cases involving legacies, intestate estates,

10

and orphans. Cases could be taken on appeal from these courts to the superior courts.[15]

In addition to these judicial functions, the county courts performed important administrative and executive duties. They carried out such tasks as supervising the building and maintenance of roads and bridges and administering the estates of orphans, and they appointed, or nominated for appointment by the governor, the sheriffs, constables, overseers of the roads, searchers, patrollers, inspectors, town commissioners, and nearly all other local officials. Thus, the county courts were exceedingly powerful bodies, and the justices were men of influence both locally and in provincial politics. Usually about two-thirds of the members of the assembly were justices of the peace, so that an alliance existed between the political leadership of the colony and the local "courthouse rings."

This alliance resulted in the perpetuation of political control in the hands of the same powerful men or families on both the local and provincial levels. The justices were appointed by the governor, but on the basis of nominations submitted to him by the local representatives in the legislature. The justices, in turn, controlled the appointment of the most powerful of all the county officials, the sheriff. The sheriff was appointed by the governor, but except in unusual cases from a list of three names submitted to him by the county justices. From 1739, when the office of sheriff was created in North Carolina, to 1745 these nominees, by law, all had to be justices of the peace, though the appointee could not function as a justice during his tenure as sheriff. After 1745 any freeholder who was not a member of the council or assembly could be nominated for the sheriff's post, but more often than not the justices nominated fellow justices. Though the justices had to nominate three men for the office, they could almost always secure the appointment of the man of their choice: sometimes they submitted the names of two men whom they knew would not accept the office along with that of their choice, whom they knew would accept; at other times they simply disregarded the law and submitted only one name. Though the governor made the appointment, in nine cases out of ten it was the local "courthouse ring" which selected the man. And it was the sheriff who conducted and supervised elections! Thus, county representatives in the legislature named the justices, the justices named the sheriffs, and the sheriffs—due to the poorly regulated and open manner in which elections were conducted—were in a position to exercise great influence over the election of representatives. It is little wonder that under this system fraud, corruption, and coercion were commonplace and that

11

"courthouse rings" were able to perpetuate themselves and dominate local politics in their own interest.

Not only could the sheriffs exercise an inordinate influence over elections, but they were extremely influential in most other areas of county government. They were the executive officers of the county courts and in theory, at least, the representatives of the crown in the counties. They were the principal peace officers in the counties and, in addition, had extensive fiscal powers. They were the collectors of colony, county, and parish taxes, and in most counties served also as vendue masters. Thus, they had countless opportunities for embezzlement and other forms of corruption leading to personal gain, and many sheriffs availed themselves of these opportunities with impunity.[16]

The widespread extent of financial corruption on the part of the sheriffs is manifest in the records of the royal period. "The sheriffs have embezzled more than one-half of the public money ordered to be raised and collected by them (about £40,000) . . . not £5,000 of which will possibly ever come into the Treasury, as in many instances the Sheriffs are either insolvent or retreated out of the Province," wrote Governor William Tryon in 1767.[17] By this time even the assembly could no longer ignore the situation, and in an act passed in 1768 it sought to curb the extent of abuse, but to little avail. In the following year it authorized a thorough investigation of the fiscal condition of the province, and in December, 1770, John Burgwyn, clerk of the court of chancery and secretary to the council, who conducted the investigation, issued his first report. It showed an outstanding indebtedness to the colony on the part of the sheriffs of £64,013 13s. 3d., a sum that exceeded by over £3,000 the total amount of taxes collected since 1748. In March, 1773, a second report indicated that the sheriffs were still in arrears £52,455 1s. 7d., and that most of the old accounts listed in the first report remained unpaid and in some cases had even increased.

Financial corruption on the part of the sheriffs was by no means due to their being underpaid, for they were among the best paid officials in the colony, deriving their income from several sources: fees for making arrests and carrying out orders of the court; commissions for collecting taxes; salaries paid by both the colony and the county (the latter for "extraordinary" services for which no fees were allowed); commissions on estates they sold as vendue masters; and other fees and commissions for administering the estates of orphans, acting as county inspectors (though this practice was eventually barred), and serving as militia officers, often as colonel of the county regiment. Because of their close ties with the county "courthouse rings," the sheriffs often also held other official positions from which they derived income, such as deputy surveyor or collector of quitrents.[18] Multiple officeholding, in fact, was one of the characteristics of county government in North Carolina. Like the sheriffs, the justices also usually held other lucrative offices.

The sheriffs were thus an important part of the fiscal system of royal North Carolina. This system was controlled by the lower house, though the governor and council, by virtue of the checks they had upon the lower house, had some control over its operation. But the lower house framed and initiated all appropriations bills, all tax legislation, and all bills providing for the issuance of currency. It also appointed and controlled the public treasurers, of which there were two, one for the northern and one for the southern half of the colony.[19] Actually, due to the influence they had with the legislators, the sheriffs had great weight in determining the selection of the treasurers. For this reason, apparently, the sheriffs were rarely sued by the treasurers over their delinquent tax accounts. That, at least, was Governor Tryon's view of the matter: "The Treasurer's lenity or rather remissness in the material part of their duty I construe to be founded on a principal of caution," he wrote in 1767, "for by not suing the sheriffs in arrears they obtain a considerable weight of interest among the connections of these delinquent sheriffs & which generally secures them a reelection in their office when expired."[20]

In operation, the fiscal system was cumbersome, inefficient, and as we have seen, shot through with corruption. The principal sources of revenue were poll and land taxes, land sales, customs duties on the importation of liquors, tonnage duties, and quitrents. Customs and tonnage duties were collected by customs collectors who received their appointments and were responsible to the commissioners of the customs in London; quitrents by sheriffs and certain territorial officers. Countless opportunities for embezzlement existed in the collection of quitrents, too, and in general they were poorly collected and constituted only a small portion of the government's income.[21]

Government revenues from quitrents were even less than they might have been due to the existence of the Granville District. This district, which constituted the entire northern half of the province— by far the wealthiest and most populous half—remained a propriety grant throughout the royal period, and all revenues from the occupation of land went not to the government, but to the proprietor. When the crown sought to purchase the interest of the Carolina proprietors in 1728, one of them, Lord Carteret, later Earl of Granville, was reluctant to sell, and the crown permitted him to retain his property rights in his one-eighth share, though he had to surrender his political rights. The boundaries of his district were later defined as the Virginia line on the north and 35° 34' on the south. The land between, a sixty-mile swath extending from the sea to the mountains, was more fertile than that to the south and contained about two-thirds of the colony's population. The crown thus assumed the expense of government in the Granville District while forfeiting all quitrents—perhaps two-thirds of the income from quitrents that the colony could produce.

Granville established his own territorial system in his district, over which neither the crown nor the provincial government exercised any control, and this was to be a prolonged source of trouble in the colony. He appointed his own land agents, surveyors, entry takers, quitrent collectors, and other officials, many of whom were dishonest and cheated both the people and Granville himself. Land agents often granted the same land to as many as three persons, charging a fee for each entry; sometimes two agents granted identical land to different persons; on occasion sheriffs, in return for bribes, granted lands that had already been taken up and changed the names of the holders in the entry books; quitrent collectors frequently charged exorbitant quitrents, and surveyors, excessive fees. It was common practice for both the land agents and the quitrent collectors to line their pockets with revenues due the proprietor. During the 1740s and 1750s, in consequence, complaints of fraud and extortion were rife in the district. In the latter decade, they were directed particularly at Francis Corbin and Thomas Child, the attorney general, both of whom were land agents for Granville, and in 1759 and 1760 rioting and other disturbances occurred in Edgecombe, Granville, and Halifax counties. Though overt resistance to Granville's representatives subsided during the 1760s, the administration of the district remained a source of vexation to the provincial government and of discontent to its inhabitants until the outbreak of the Revolution.[22]

The trouble over the administration of the Granville District was but a prelude to the eruption of even more serious strife in the same general region less than a decade later, caused primarily by corruption and abuse of the people by county officials (as distinguished from Granville's territorial agents). Resistance to this new incidence of corruption on the part of the "courthouse rings" found expression and organization in the regulator movement of 1765-1771, which had its nucleus in Orange County but derived substantial support from other western and piedmont counties, including Granville, Rowan,

14

Edgecombe, Anson, Halifax, Johnston, and Dobbs.

The regulators charged specifically that sheriffs, local justices, and other county officials extracted exorbitant fees from the people, committed fraud and extortion in the collection of taxes and rents, confiscated private goods for tax payments in lieu of money, and embezzled public funds. At the heart of the trouble was the developing sectionalism between east and west, deriving from the more populous western counties being unfairly represented in the assembly, and the system of local government, described earlier, in which self-perpetuating "courthouse rings" in league with the eastern-controlled assembly maintained domination over local affairs. But to the people of the western counties the direct cause of their distress was the malfeasance of their officials. As a protest from Granville County expressed it: "it is not our mode or form of Government, nor yet the body of our laws, that we are quarreling with, but with the malpractices of the Officers of our County Courts, and the abuses which we suffer by those empowered to manage our public affairs. . . ." [23]

The regulators tried repeatedly to get the assembly to redress their grievances, but without success, and the continued abuses led to intermittent disturbances, mob protests, and even rioting in Orange and to a lesser extent in Edgecombe, Anson, and Johnston counties between 1768 and 1771. Conditions became so turbulent, in fact, that in January, 1771, the legislature passed a harsh, repressive measure called the Johnston Riot Act, named for its author, Samuel Johnston, who soon was to become a principal leader in the colony's revolutionary movement. Under the act, if ten or more persons "unlawfully, tumultuously and riotously assembled together" and refused to disperse within an hour after being ordered to do so they would be charged with committing a felony and, if found guilty, condemned to death. If an accused but unapprehended person did not surrender within sixty days he would be considered guilty, and anyone might kill him with impunity. The act also authorized the governor to suppress future riots or insurrections by military force.

The regulators were enraged at this measure and responded to it with defiance. They denounced the act, pledged themselves to pay no further taxes until it was repealed, declared Edmund Fanning, a notoriously corrupt local official who had long been a target of regulator wrath, to be an outlaw who might be killed on sight, forbade the holding of court sessions, and threatened death to all lawyers and judges. Governor Tryon, with the support of both council and assembly, now took dramatic action. He called a special session of court to convene at Hillsborough, Orange County, in March, 1771, and then summoned the militia to protect the court and suppress the Regulation. Assuming command personally, he led his force of about 1,500 men, over two-thirds of them easterners, to Alamance Creek, a few miles west of Hillsborough. Determined to resist force by force, the regulators gathered some 2,000 men and marched to Alamance Creek, where they confronted Tryon's army. The ensuing battle resulted in the defeat and dispersal of the regulators and the collapse of their cause. Twelve of their leaders were convicted of treason, and though six of these were later pardoned, six were hanged, and hundreds of regulators fled westward into the Tennessee country. Tryon then promised clemency to all who would agree to submit to government, and nearly 6,500 did so. They were pardoned by the king during the administration of Tryon's successor, Josiah Martin.

The regulator movement was a violent manifestation of western discontent over the malpractices of corrupt and sometimes oppressive local officials, many of whom had close connections in the eastern-dominated colonial legislature. That body had no sympathy for the regulators' cause, was full of anger and vengeance at their resistance to law and authority, and many of its members participated personally in the suppression of the revolt at Alamance. As a result, thousands of backcountry people bore lasting antipathy toward the eastern leaders and continuing resentment over the assembly's neglect of western interests, and when the revolutionary movement got under way a few years later under the leadership of the very men who had opposed their cause, they viewed it as means by which these traditional enemies could increase and perpetuate their power to the great disadvantage of the people of the west. This resentment and fear was doubtless an important influence in persuading large numbers in this region to remain actively or passively loyal to the crown during the ensuing struggle with Britain.[24]

II

Congresses and Committees:
The Defiance of Royal Authority

Shortly after the suppression of the Regulation at Alamance, Governor Tryon left North Carolina to become royal governor of New York. At the time of his departure he was on exceedingly good terms with the assembly. That body had supported him wholeheartedly in his campaign against the regulators, and no controversies had arisen in succeeding months to prejudice relations between them. Charming, diplomatic, and a skillful political manager, Tryon, in fact, had gotten on well with the assembly during most of his administration. That is not to say that very serious problems had not arisen during the course of it. Indeed, no sooner had he assumed office in 1765 than the Stamp Act crisis shook the province.

Opposition to the Stamp Act—which taxed newspapers, licenses, cards, dice, legal documents, and the like—was vigorous and determined in North Carolina. Demonstrations against the act occurred in several towns and counties during the summer and fall of 1765, and at Wilmington, on the Cape Fear, where feeling was particularly intense, the Sons of Liberty organized to resist the act. Mass meetings attended by as many as 500 people protested the stamps around blazing bonfires on two occasions in October, and on November 16 a mob numbering close to 400 forced the stamp agent, Dr. William Houston, to resign his commission. Twelve days later an armed body of men met the sloop *Diligence* on its arrival at Brunswick and prevented the landing of North Carolina's first consignment of stamps. In retaliation Governor Tryon banned all further business in the courts, and the *Diligence*, joined shortly by another British ship, the *Viper*, blocked all ships from entering or clearing the Cape Fear River that did not have stamps on their papers. The result was the virtual stoppage of legal transactions in the province and the near strangulation of trade. When in January and early February, 1766, three ships attempted to enter the Cape Fear with unstamped clearance papers, the *Viper* seized them, and the attorney general of the province, Robert Jones, determined to bring proceedings against them at Halifax, Nova Scotia, rather than at Cape Fear. This highly unpopular decision produced still another mass meeting attended by men from all the lower Cape Fear counties (Duplin, Bladen, New Hanover, and Brunswick) who adopted an "association" pledging themselves "at any risque whatever, and whenever called upon, [to] unite, and truly and faithfully assist each other . . . in preventing entirely the operation of the Stamp Act." They also created an armed force of some 600 men which, together with nearly 400 unarmed men, marched to Brunswick, seized the customs house, forced the captain of the *Viper* to release the vessels and promise to make no further attempt to enforce the Stamp Act, and compelled the collector, controller, clerks, and other public officials who could be found to swear an oath that they would perform no duty relating to the act. Thus ended the enforcement of the Stamp Act in North Carolina.[1]

Governor Tryon, meanwhile, had refused to call the assembly into session in time for it to appoint delegates to the Stamp Act Congress in New York, for which he was reprimanded by the assembly when he finally convened it in 1766. With the repeal of the Stamp Act by Parliament in March, however, conditions in the colony returned to normal. The legislature again entered into amicable relations with the governor, trade resumed, and public business proceeded. Quickly the province turned its attention from imperial problems to domestic concerns, and in particular, to the rising agitation amongst the regulators in the west. Not until late 1769 did executive-legislative relations become strained once more, and as before an imperial issue, this time the Townshend Revenue Act, was the source of controversy.

Though the Revenue Act went into effect in November, 1767, there was little reaction to it in North Carolina until a year later, and then the opposition that developed was neither strong nor unified. Although the constitutional issue—the right of Parliament to tax the colonies for revenue purposes—was identical with that raised by the Stamp Act, most North Carolinians at this stage of the controversy with Britain showed as little concern for constitutional principles as for economic effects. The stamp tax, after all, bore directly upon nearly every citizen of the colony, and it was passed during a year of poor harvests and unusual economic hardship. The Townshend Revenue Act, on the other hand, imposed duties on only a few items of colonial import—glass, paper, lead pigments, and tea—and these would be borne directly by the merchants, only indirectly, if at all, by the average citizen. Moreover, commerce in North Carolina was of secondary importance, and the act would have far less effect there than in the northern commercial colonies. Clearly, the Townshend Revenue Act seemed far less ominous to most North Carolinians than the Stamp Act had appeared to be, and they reacted accordingly.

18

English cartoon about the repeal of the Stamp Act on March 18, 1766. The funeral procession features George Grenville, architect of the stamp tax, carrying the coffin of Miss Americ-Stamp into a vault over which the skeleton heads bear the dates of two Scottish rebellions, 1715 and 1745. From Donald H. Cresswell, comp., *The American Revolution in Drawings and Prints* (Washington: Library of Congress, 1975), 243, hereinafter cited as *The Revolution in Drawings and Prints.*

The North Carolina legislature took no action regarding the Revenue Act until November, 1768, a year after it had gone into effect. Then the occasion for action was the introduction of a spirited communication from the Massachusetts legislature—the Massachusetts Circular Letter of February 11, 1768. Composed by Samuel Adams, the letter branded the Townshend Revenue Act an unconstitutional measure and called upon the colonies to join Massachusetts in a concerted defense of colonial rights. Actually, the letter had been received by the speaker of the North Carolina house, John Harvey, on April 1, but the house did not take it under consideration during the remainder of that session, which was concluded by prorogation at the end of the month. When the house reconvened in November, however, it issued verbal instructions to the speaker to answer the letter, and three weeks later it finally resolved to petition the king for a repeal of the Townshend duties. The petition, adopted December 5, denounced the duties as unconstitutional and condemned any sort of parliamentary taxation for revenue purposes.[2]

Opposition to the Townshend acts, meanwhile, had taken much more vigorous form in New England and New York, where beginning in August, 1768, merchant associations agreed to limit the importation of British goods and to boycott completely the items taxed until the Revenue Act was repealed.[3] Such developments did not occur in the southern colonies until much later. Less adversely affected by the duties and the other Townshend measures, southern merchants were

19

unwilling to pursue a course that would be financially damaging. By May, 1769, however, Virginia was roused to greater action by further British measures, notably the stationing of four regiments of red-coats in Boston to maintain order and enforce the Revenue Act and Parliament's encouragement of the ministry to transport the leaders of the resistance in Massachusetts to England for trial. When news of these developments arrived in Virginia, the burgesses registered their repugnance in unequivocal terms. On May 17 they unanimously ap-proved resolutions denouncing taxation without representation, defending the issuance of the Massachusetts Circular Letter, and asserting the right of Virginians charged with treason to be tried in Virginia. The next day, in an address to the king, they condemned as unconstitutional the transportation of Americans to England for trial. The governor thereupon dissolved the house, but the members shortly removed to a private home, where as private citizens they en-tered into a nonimportation association.[4]

In the meantime, North Carolina's leaders had taken no action against the Townshend acts beyond their December protest to the crown, and the province had remained quiet. The parliamentary measures that aroused the Virginia burgesses and their vigorous response, however, promoted a rising spirit of opposition to the southward. The North Carolina legislature was not in session when the Virginia resolutions were passed, but shortly after it convened late in October it virtually duplicated the action of the Virginia burgesses. On November 2 it unanimously adopted a series of resolu-tions and an address to the king nearly identical with those of Virginia. At once Governor Tryon dissolved the house, and after the Virginia example all but three of its sixty-seven members removed to the courthouse where in the course of a two-day session they drew up and adopted a nonimportation association.[5]

Following this extralegal action several local associations were adopted, but apparently little effort was made to enforce them, ex-cept on the Cape Fear, and even there enforcement was incomplete. According to Tryon, the nonimportation movement in North Carolina was a near total failure. "Notwithstanding the boasted associations of people who never were in trade," he wrote in 1771, "and the sham patriotism of a few merchants to the southward of the province, the several ports of this province have been open ever since the repeal of the Stamp Act for every kind of British manufactures to the full ex-tent of the credit of the country." One probable difficulty in es-tablishing effective enforcement—apart from the reluctance of many North Carolina merchants to comply—lay in the fact that by the time the provincial nonimportation association was adopted the rumor was already widespread that Parliament would soon repeal all of the duties except the one on tea. In May, 1769, an announcement that the ministry would request such action from Parliament had issued to the colonies, and in his October address to the assembly Governor Tryon had urged the members to pursue a moderate course (advice which, as we have seen, they did not heed) in view of the ministry's announced intentions. On March 5, 1770, just four months after the adoption of the North Carolina nonimportation agreement, Parliament complied with the ministry's request and repealed all duties except the tea duty. It thus seems likely that enforcement of nonimportation in North Carolina was hampered by rumors of repeal and by the actual repeal before it could become effective.[6]

When news of the repeal arrived in the Cape Fear region a six-county meeting of the Sons of Liberty pledged to maintain nonimportation until the tea duty was lifted, but this effort was in vain. Nonimportation was already in the process of collapse in the northern colonies, and North Carolina shortly followed their example.[7] Thus, the controversy over the Townshend acts came to an end in the province. Soon the leaders of the assembly joined with Governor Tryon in the suppression of the regulators, and the imperial issue was for the most part forgotten. It would be revived again only with Parliament's passage of the Tea Act in 1773, by which time Tryon had long since become governor of New York and his replacement in North Carolina, Josiah Martin, had already become embroiled in bitter controversy with a hostile assembly over a local issue involving the powers of the provincial courts.

Martin had had a military career prior to his assumption of the governorship in August, 1771. He therefore had no experience with and little understanding of colonial problems. He was also stubborn, blunt, impatient, and sometimes rash, and he lacked the imagination of his predecessor. But he had other qualities too. He was intelligent enough, conscientious, energetic, fair minded, honest, sincere, and completely loyal to the crown.[8] It was this last quality, in fact—manifested in his uncompromising insistence upon crown prerogative—in combination with the less favorable characteristics of his personality, that produced in the assembly a growing hostility toward him. Probably no colonial governor could have gotten on well with that body in the three or four years prior to the Revolution, but under a more skillful and diplomatic governor executive-legislative relations might have been less critical and the court controversy of 1773-1774 less productive of discontent in the province.

From the outset of his administration Martin got along poorly with the assembly. In 1771 he aroused its ire by denouncing as illegal and in violation of public faith a measure of the assembly discontinuing the sinking fund tax, which had been levied several years earlier to redeem outstanding bills of credit. When, despite his protests, the assembly refused to continue the tax, he ordered the sheriffs to collect it anyhow. Thereupon the assembly defiantly promised to indemnify all officers who suffered because they refused to comply with his order. In 1772 executive-legislative relations worsened when Martin, on instruction from the crown, ordered the continuation of a

A reproduction of the crest of the coat of arms of royal Governor Josiah Martin, commissioned in 1962 by Tryon Palace, New Bern.

boundary survey between North and South Carolina that resulted in the loss to the former of thousands of acres of land. So angered was the assembly that it refused to pay for the survey.[9] In the same year Martin further damaged his popularity with the legislature when he toured the regulator country, listening sympathetically to the grievances of participants in the rebellion. He became convinced of the justice of their cause and promised to use his influence with the crown to secure their pardon. The result of his efforts was a crown recommendation in 1773 that the assembly grant amnesty to the regulators, a recommendation that the assembly rejected, ostensibly

22

because the proposal failed to except certain regulator leaders. Martin also sought to expose corrupt officials who had preyed upon the regulators, many of whom had close ties with the assembly. In consequence, wrote a former regulator leader, "our officers hate him as bad as we hated Tryon, only they don't speak so free."[10] Not until 1773, however, did the developing resentment of Martin contribute to a crisis of serious proportions—the court controversy, which precipitated the agitation and organization that culminated in North Carolina's revolt against Britain.

The controversy began in February when the assembly presented Martin with a bill continuing and amending the superior and inferior court laws of 1767, which were due to expire. Martin rejected the bill, primarily because it contained a clause empowering the courts to attach the North Carolina property of defaulting debtors living in England. This clause, which had been included in the act of 1767, was opposed by British merchants, many of whom transacted business in North Carolina and owned land there, and the crown had instructed Martin not to consent to any new bill containing it. The legislature now adopted a compromise bill that contained the "attachments clause" but provided that the law would not take effect until it had been approved by the crown. To this measure Martin reluctantly assented.

To provide for the immediate need for courts in the colony, however, the lower house passed two temporary bills establishing superior and inferior courts for a period of six months, but these bills also contained the attachments clause, and the council so amended them as to nullify that forbidden provision. Controversy now broke out between the two houses. At length, the council passed the inferior court bill with the attachments clause intact, but it refused to budge on the superior court bill. Martin now vetoed the inferior court bill and at the same time rejected sixteen other bills and prorogued the legislature for three days in the apparent hope that his action would make the members more compliant. It had the opposite effect. Most members left immediately for home, and when the legislature was due to convene on March 9, only fifteen appeared to take their seats— less than a quorum—and the session could not be continued. Martin thereupon dissolved the assembly and issued a call for the election of a new one, which was to convene May 1. With the dissolution of this assembly the judicial system of North Carolina collapsed; not a single court existed in the colony and no provision had been made for any.

Martin now exercised his authority under the royal prerogative to create courts of oyer and terminer and general jail delivery in order to enforce the criminal law and preserve order, and during the summer sessions of the courts of oyer and terminer were held in several counties. Perhaps apprehensive of the reaction of the assembly to his creation of these courts, however, Martin prorogued it from time to time until December, 1773, when he finally allowed it to meet.[11] Meanwhile, he received in late summer the expected royal disallowance of the compromise court act of February, and in his address to the new assembly in December he informed it of that fact. At the same time he called upon the members to pass an acceptable court law and requested funds for the maintenance of the courts of oyer and terminer that he had established. To the latter request the house responded sharply and with finality. It unanimously rejected the request on the ground that such courts could not "be legally carried into execution without the aid of the Legislature of this Province, and that we cannot consistent with the Justice due to our Constituents make provisions for defraying the expense attending a measure which we do not approve."[12]

The house then drew up a new court bill, but it, too, contained the attachments clause, and the council rejected it. Thereupon the house appointed a committee to draft an address to the king setting forth the colony's position on the attachments clause. The committee was also directed to write to Tryon, in New York, asking him to present the address to the king and to support it "with his interest and influence." Tryon was to be informed that the assembly's request was "testimony of the great affection this Colony bears him, and the entire confidence they repose in him." Little short of an outright insult, this resolution persuaded Governor Martin that he could do nothing with the assembly for the present, and he prorogued it until March 1. The session thus ended without a single act having been passed.[13]

The refusal of the assembly to appropriate funds to maintain the courts of oyer and terminer brought about their collapse, and in ensuing months there were neither civil nor criminal courts in the province, a grave situation that produced widespread discontent. In the eastern counties most people apparently blamed Governor Martin and British policy for the situation. Here the leaders of the assembly were especially influential, and they stirred up much popular support for their position. In so doing, they contributed substantially to the growth of anti-British sentiment by the spring of 1774. In the piedmont counties, where during the Revolution loyalism was to be strong, the people were less inclined to blame the governor and the British and prone to attribute responsibility to the eastern politicians. In the far western counties the closing of the courts created much dissatisfaction, but there, too, many were inclined to blame the eastern political leaders. In the piedmont and west, therefore, the court controversy was apparently less influential in promoting anti-British feeling than in the east, where it was of major importance.[14]

When the legislature convened again in March, 1774, the permanent court law was the crucial issue. Governor Martin made an earnest appeal to the delegates to discard the attachments clause, but to no avail, and he again exercised his veto. The assembly did pass temporary acts establishing inferior courts and courts of oyer and terminer, however, and Martin reluctantly assented to them. But the establishment of superior courts was another matter. That problem could not be solved, even on a temporary basis, and on March 25 Martin prorogued the assembly until May 25. On March 24, however, the assembly again resolved that the one shilling poll tax for the redemption of outstanding bills of credit should not be collected. When Martin heard this news he could not contain his anger, and on March 30 he issued a sharply worded proclamation dissolving the assembly.[15] Before a new one met, the colony was in the process of revolt, and the court question had become submerged in larger and even more acrimonious imperial issues.

It might seem strange that the attachments question produced such a furor in North Carolina, for the debts owed by Englishmen to North Carolinians were not extensive, and therefore the right of attachment was not nearly as important to the welfare of the colony as the assembly pretended. But the attachments controversy was the culminating battle in the long struggle for legislative supremacy and provincial autonomy, and it was intensified by the legislature's deepening dislike of Martin as well as by the simultaneous escalation of general colonial opposition to British authority.[16]

Indeed, at the time the court controversy began there was already in existence in the North Carolina lower house a radical, anti-imperial faction, several members of which had been leaders in the agitation against Parliament during the preceding decade. Among these were John Harvey, Samuel Johnston, and Joseph Hewes of the Albemarle region, Isaac Edwards and Richard Cogdell of New Bern, and Cornelius Harnett, Robert Howe, William Hooper, and John Ashe of the Cape Fear area. Josiah Quincy, Jr., in March, 1773, noted the existence of such a faction, "a select number who had mutually agreed and solemnly promised each other to keep each a regular journal not only of the public occurrences, but of the conduct of every public character."[17] Visiting North Carolina to urge the establishment of a provincial committee of correspondence, as recommended by the

Virginia burgesses in a recent circular letter to the colonies, Quincy was well pleased with the Carolinians' reaction, for he found that the whig leaders received the proposal with enthusiasm. He had arrived in the province at just the right time, of course, for just two weeks earlier the assembly had been locked in heated controversy with the governor over the court law, Martin had ordered a dissolution, and the members had returned home in an angry and defiant mood. No wonder that the Virginia proposal had appeal! No action could be taken with regard to it until the assembly met again in December, however. At that time the Virginia letter urging interprovincial committees was presented to the house, which proceeded immediately to appoint one. Thus, the assembly, which refused to pass a single act requested by the governor—and passed no others, for that matter—acted to bring North Carolina more directly into cooperation with the other colonies in the continental resistance movement against Britain.[18]

To the committee of correspondence the house appointed nine men, all residents of the eastern counties, all men of property and position with substantial political experience in the assembly and at the local level, all champions of colonial "rights" who were to play leading roles in the ensuing revolutionary struggle, and most of them leaders in the assembly's struggle against Martin in the court controversy and in the provincial opposition to Parliament and the ministry during the preceding decade. Included were John Harvey of Perquimans County, speaker of the house, wealthy planter, and militia colonel; Samuel Johnston of Chowan, planter, lawyer, real estate magnate; Richard Caswell of Dobbs, lawyer, planter, speculator, militia colonel and owner of a large landed estate; Cornelius Harnett of Wilmington, planter, merchant, shipowner; Joseph Hewes of Edenton, leading merchant, shipowner, and planter; William Hooper of New Hanover, Harvard graduate, lawyer, and substantial planter; John Ashe of New Hanover, former speaker of the house, wealthy planter, and leader of the opposition to the Stamp Act on the Cape Fear; Robert Howe of Brunswick, militia colonel who had long served as commander of Fort Johnston at the mouth of the Cape Fear, and one of the wealthiest planters in the province; and Edward Vail of Chowan, planter and colonel in the militia.[19] With the appointment of this committee the stage was set for the initiation of the revolutionary movement in North Carolina, and the first step had been taken in the formation of its revolutionary government.

The second step in that process came in the summer of 1774 with the calling of the first of five extralegal provincial congresses held over the next two and one-half years—the principal agencies through which the difficult transition from royal to state government was achieved. Actually, an attempt had been made by John Harvey, chairman of the committee of correspondence as well as speaker of the house, to call a provincial congress into session in early April, 1774. By that time the bitter legislative-executive struggle over the court law plus the contagious colonial resentment over parliamentary interference in colonial affairs, recently inflamed anew by the Tea Act, had produced considerable dissatisfaction and unrest in the province. Reflecting that discontent and frustration and furious at the reported refusal of Martin to convene an assembly "until he had some chance of a better one than the last," Harvey sought the support of the other members of the committee of correspondence in calling a provincial congress into session without executive sanction. He secured the support of Willie Jones, wealthy assembly leader of Halifax town, and Samuel Johnston. Johnston immediately informed William Hooper of the plan and called upon him to enlist the aid of Cornelius Harnett and John Ashe, "or any other such men."[20] But the proposed congress did not materialize. Practical considerations undoubtedly worked against it. The leaders must have decided that popular animosity against Britain was not yet strong enough in the province to provide an unlawful congress with sufficient support. They may also have been wary of taking such a risky step in the absence of similar proceedings in the other colonies.

If these were the reasons why the call for a congress did not issue, their force was soon diminished by the reaction in the colonies to Parliament's passage of the Boston Port Bill. Designed to punish Boston for its indulgence in the Tea Party, together with the other Coercive Acts it fanned the flames of resistance from New Hampshire to Georgia and led to the calling of the First Continental Congress. Virginia's reaction to the Port Bill had special influence upon the course pursued by North Carolina's whig leaders. When the news of it arrived at Williamsburg, the House of Burgesses proclaimed a fast day in honor of the people of Boston, whereupon the governor dissolved the house on May 25, 1774. The burgesses then reconvened extralegally at the Raleigh Tavern, where they adopted a boycott association against British commerce, proposed a general colonial congress, and issued a call for the election of delegates to a provincial congress to meet at Williamsburg on August 1.[21]

When tidings of these events reached the North Carolina Committee of Correspondence on June 9, it took immediate action. Within a day it met, approved the stand taken by Virginia, and dispatched a

The closing of the port of Boston prompted this London mezzotint, dated November 19, 1774, showing distressed Bostonians trapped in a cage hanging from a Liberty Tree. From *The Revolution in Drawings and Prints*, 276.

message to the South Carolina Committee of Correspondence strongly supporting Virginia's measures. The committee indicated its belief, moreover, that North Carolina would cooperate in a boycott on trade with Britain and in such additional measures as the colonies in general agreed upon if the Port Bill was not repealed. Though it could not be absolutely certain that its position coincided with that of the general public, the committee believed that the people would indicate their support "whenever they have an opportunity."[22]

The committee was obviously hampered by the fact that the assembly was not in session. It was difficult to know just how far North Carolinians would go in support of the Virginia patriots until the representatives of the counties and towns had voiced their sentiments. Concern over this problem was reflected in the committee's reply to Virginia. After strongly endorsing the burgesses' measures, the committee continued:

> We had been happy, if we had been fully authorized to speak the general sense of the people of this province. Be assured that we will, with all possible expedition, use the best means to obtain it. Should not our Assembly meet on the 26th of July, to which time it now stands prorogued, we shall endeavor in some other manner to collect the Representatives of the people and shall immediately afterwards transmit to you . . . the result of their deliberations. . . . They will, we flatter ourselves, concur with you that the best expedient to bring about a reconciliation with the mother Country . . . will be to put a stop to all commercial Intercourse with her and the West Indies. . . .[23]

28

Though anxious to bring together the representatives of the people, the committee thus decided against issuing an immediate call for a revolutionary congress. Apparently still uncertain as to how such a call would be received by the people, it determined to allow the governor an opportunity to convene the lawful assembly. The committee continued to lay plans against the eventuality that the governor would refuse to act, however, and it probably suspected at the outset that this would be the case. But the committee decided against assuming direct responsibility for calling a congress, for the call, when it came, issued from a mass meeting at Wilmington of freeholders from six counties in the Cape Fear region.[24]

The Wilmington meeting, held on July 21 and led by William Hooper, sounded the keynote of rebellion in North Carolina. Inflamed by patriot propaganda, by the Port Bill and the other Coercive Acts, and encouraged by news of radical proceedings in other colonies, the freeholders denounced the recent measures of Parliament and issued a call to the people of all the counties in the province to send delegates to a provincial congress to be held on August 20 at Johnston County Courthouse. (The date and place were later changed to August 25 at New Bern.) The purpose of the congress would be to consider "the present alarming state of British America and in concert with the other Colonies . . . adopt and prosecute such measures as will most effectually tend to avert the miseries" under which the colonies suffered. One such measure, it was stressed, should be the holding of a continental congress at which delegates of the several colonies might adopt a "uniform plan for the conduct of all North America." The "cause of . . . Boston," the freeholders asserted, was the "common cause of British America," and they agreed to send supplies to the Bostonians "as an earnest of our sincere Intentions to contribute by every means in our power to alleviate their distress and to enduce them to maintain . . . the glorious cause in which they at present suffer."[25]

In the month following the Wilmington meeting similar proceedings occurred in most of the counties of the province and in most towns that ordinarily sent delegates to the assembly. The records of only eight such meetings are extant,[26] but many more must have been held, for thirty of the colony's thirty-five counties, and six towns, sent delegates to the provincial congress, which convened on August 25 at New Bern.

The atmosphere that day must have been charged with unusual excitement, for the congress had been called extralegally and the delegates extralegally elected. They had come to act upon a momentous proposition: that North Carolina should take united action with the other colonies in overt resistance to Britain. There were seventy-one delegates in attendance, including the eight members of the committee of correspondence, who doubtless assumed the leadership of the congress. John Harvey, chairman of the committee and speaker of the regular assembly, was unanimously chosen moderator. Under his guidance the congress finished its work in less than three days.

The congress concerned itself in the main with drawing up a series of resolutions that aired the grievances of the colonists against Parliament and committed North Carolina to a policy of united resistance with the other colonies. The resolutions were prefaced by a statement in which the delegates reiterated their loyalty to the king and the Hanoverian succession, charged that the rights of the colonies had been "invaded by powers unwarrantably assumed by Parliament," and explained that a desire to declare their sentiments "in the most public manner" had prompted the meeting of the congress, "lest silence . . . be construed as acquiescence, and that we patiently submit to the Burdens which they have thought fit to impose upon us." Turning to specific grievances, the delegates condemned parliamentary taxation of the colonists as contrary to their rights as Englishmen and as repugnant to the British constitution and asserted that only the colonial assemblies possessed that right. The duties imposed by Parliament on tea and other commodities imported into America were therefore "highly illegal and oppressive." By resisting them, the people of Massachusetts had "distinguished themselves in a manly support of the rights of America," and the punitive measures with which Parliament had responded were unconstitutional, cruel, unjust, and oppressive.

After expressing their conviction that colonial rights could be preserved only by united resistance, the delegates, in compliance with the request of the Boston patriots and following the lead of such colonies as Virginia, Maryland, and South Carolina, formulated and approved a positive program of action. Included was a plan of economic coercion against Britain similar to that adopted by Virginia. If the grievances of the colonists were not redressed by January 1, 1775, no goods except medicines were to be imported from Britain or the British East or West Indies. The importation of slaves was forbidden after November 1, 1774. No East India tea was to be consumed by North Carolinians after September 10, 1774, and anyone who violated this injunction was to be considered an enemy to his country. If Parliament did not repeal its objectionable measures by October 1, 1775, complete nonexportation of goods to Britain was to go into effect.

The congress next endorsed the proposed general congress of all the colonies and appointed delegates: William Hooper, Joseph Hewes, and Richard Caswell, all members of the committee of correspondence. They were invested with broad powers: "any act done by them or consent given in behalf of this province" was to be "Obligatory in honor upon every inhabitant . . . who is not an alien to his Country's good and apostate to the liberties of America." They were instructed to "view the attempt made by the ministers upon the Town of Boston, as a prelude to a general attack upon the rights of other Colonies," and to inform the Continental Congress that North Carolinians considered it their "duty to Contribute . . . to ease the burthen imposed upon that town for their Virtuous Opposition to the Revenue Acts . . . ." They were to express the loyalty of the people to the king, but at the same time emphasize the determination of North Carolinians to maintain "a firm and resolute defence of our persons and properties against all unconstitutional encroachments whatever," including that of taxation without representation. They were to inform the congress of North Carolina's determination to institute the aforementioned restrictions on trade with Britain in the event that grievances were not redressed. Finally, they were to concur with the delegates of the other colonies "in such regulation, address or remonstrance as may be deemed most probable to restore a lasting harmony . . . with Great Britain" and to agree with a majority "in all necessary measures, for promoting a redress . . . of . . . grievances."

After passing a resolution providing for the stoppage of "all trade, Commerce and dealings" with any colony, community, or person who refused to support continental measures, the provincial congress next sought to put teeth in its decrees and provide for future exigencies by bringing about more widespread and effective radical organization in the province. It passed a resolution recommending the appointment of five-member committees of safety in each of the counties to act as enforcement bodies and to correspond with the provincial committee of correspondence. Thus the provincial congress fostered the creation of local radical organizations that paralleled the existing county governments. As the Revolution developed, these local committees supplanted the county institutions as the repositories of local political authority. The whigs also provided for future meetings of the congress. John Harvey was empowered to call another session whenever he thought necessity required it. In the event of his death, Samuel Johnston was to assume this responsibility.[27]

While the congress thus drew North Carolina into the developing struggle with Britain, Governor Martin fumed and despaired. He had issued a proclamation forbidding it from meeting, but his council had advised against taking any stronger action, and some of its members may actually have sympathized with the purposes of the congress. Five of the nine active members of the council recently had sided with the lower house on the superior court issue, advising Martin to approve a bill containing the "attachments clause," advice which so angered him that he called for their removal from office. When the provincial congress was in session these same councillors went so far as to fraternize with the delegates against his express injunction and thus appeared to sympathize with their proceedings. The conduct of these council members brought home to Martin as nothing else had done the real impotence of his position in the colony.[28] The congress, it is true, had made no attempt to replace the existing administration with a revolutionary government, and theoretically Martin still retained his authority; in fact, however, whatever power he had previously exerted over the affairs of the province had now largely come to an end. From this time forward more and more power passed into the hands of the patriots and their leaders, under whose guidance the province moved with increasing certainty down the road to revolution.

For the next several months the movement was largely decentralized. The committee of correspondence provided a measure of direction and unity, but most active radical measures were local in nature and initiated by the leaders in the counties and towns. The congress had stimulated the formation of local committees of safety, and these now took complete charge of affairs in the localities where they existed. Records exist showing the formation of ten county or town committees from the time of the first congress until April, 1775, when the second congress met, but in all probability several more came into being during this period. Aside from Rowan County in the west where a powerful committee operated, most of the committee activity at this time occurred in the seaboard counties. Committees were active in each of the important coastal towns—Edenton, New Bern, and Wilmington—and in the counties of Halifax, Pitt, Duplin, Chowan, New Hanover, Bute, and Craven, the committee in the last county operating also as the committee for New Bern.[29] Their main concern was the enforcement of the decrees of the provincial and continental congresses relative to nonimportation, nonconsumption, and price regulation, but they engaged, also, in promoting home industry, in discouraging extravagance and high living, in coercing recalcitrant or unenthusiastic citizens, and in continual propaganda activity. They demanded signatures to the Association,[30] which stipulated the prohibitions on trade and conduct, and published and spread abroad the names of those who refused to sign, violated it, or in other ways injured the cause. They kept one another informed of the status of revolutionary feeling in their respective counties and endeavored to stir up antipathy against Britain by word of mouth, private letters, handbills, pamphlets, and articles and news reports in the colony's two newspapers, the *North Carolina Gazette*, published at New Bern, and the *Cape Fear Mercury*, published at Wilmington. According to Governor Martin, the committees used every conceivable device to keep the pot of revolution boiling.

> The seditious leaders of the People . . . talk of resorting to violence instead of submission [he wrote in March, 1775], and continue to prompt the people to discontent by all the most false, base and scandalous suggestions, reports and insinuations that unprincipled men can invent, which are readily swallowed by the poor deluded people whose extreme ignorance and credulity exposes them to receive every imposition that the crafty and ill designing men practice upon them with unwearied pains and diligence.[31]

Martin's statement reveals his own great indignation and frustration over the state of affairs in the province, but it indicates, also, that the propaganda activities of the committees had a powerful effect in bolstering the revolutionary cause.

Another important activity of the committees was the collection of goods for the relief of Boston. Actually, the radical leaders had initiated vigorous steps to collect supplies for the Bostonians upon first learning of the passage of the Coercive Acts. In consequence, by the end of July the Wilmington committee was able to ship to Boston £800 worth of provisions contributed by the people of the Cape Fear area, and in September the Edenton committee dispatched a ship to Boston with nearly 2,100 bushels of corn, 22 barrels of flour, and 17 barrels of pork collected from nearby counties. In early 1775 the New Bern and Pitt County committees also prepared to send cargoes of goods to Massachusetts.[32]

These manifestations of public support for the radical cause—the contribution of supplies to Boston, the widespread adoption of the Association, the formation and activities of the county and town committees—suggest the growing strength of the revolutionary movement in North Carolina in the period between the First and Second Provincial congresses, though, as previously indicated, public ardor was considerably more intense in the eastern counties than in the backcountry. The Cape Fear region, spreading out from Wilmington, was especially rebellious. "As to public matters I shall . . . please you, when I inform you that a patriotick spirit possesses every bosom, which all ranks of persons seem emulous to express, by actions as well as words," wrote one observer in August, 1774; "there is apparent in almost every individual a proper sense of the injury done to the Colonies, in the tendency of those oppressive Acts of Parliament, and a determined spirit of opposition and resentment worthy of a human bosom in the great cause of liberty."[33] When a Scottish lady, Janet Schaw, visited the Cape Fear area several months later she was so shocked at the prevailing radicalism that she attributed to the men of the area a "natural ferocity" that now had been "inflamed by the fury of an ignorant zeal." She could not even look at them "without connecting the idea of tar and feather."[34] With the meeting of the Second Provincial Congress and, shortly thereafter, arrival of the news of Lexington and Concord, rebellious ardor took even greater possession of the seaboard area and inspired, as well, more and more people in the piedmont and western parts of the colony, though these areas were to remain infested with loyalists and with the apathetic throughout the Revolution.

John Harvey issued the call for the Second Provincial Congress on February 11, 1775. His purpose was to insure that a body of representatives from the counties and towns met in time to appoint delegates to the Second Continental Congress, which was scheduled to convene on May 10. Since the General Assembly stood prorogued until late in March and might well be prorogued again, there was danger that no delegates would be chosen unless the representatives were brought together extralegally for this purpose.[35] When Governor Martin learned of the proposed congress, however, he sought to discourage it from meeting by permitting the General Assembly to convene at the end of March, as scheduled, and on March 6 he issued a strongly worded proclamation against the congress:

> ... Whereas the Assembly of this Province duly elected is the only true and lawful Representation of the People and is competent to every legal Act that Representatives of the people can do, and as an attempt to excite the people to choose another body of Representatives to meet at the time and place appointed for the meeting of the Assembly is to betray them in a violation of the Constitution, . . . to support it [the congress] a contempt of that branch of the Legislature which represents the People . . . I do hereby earnestly exhort the . . . People . . . that they do . . . steadfastly persevere in . . . loyal and dutiful conduct, and continue to resist and treat with just indignation all measures so subversive to Order and Government. . . .

The people, moreover, should refuse to subject themselves to "Tyrannical and arbitrary Committees," and "renounce, disclaim and discourage all such meetings cabals and illegal proceedings which artful and designing men shall attempt to engage them in." [36]

Martin's proclamation perhaps had some effect, for nine of the thirty-five counties returned no representatives to the congress, while only five had failed to send representatives to the First Provincial Congress. Moreover, Martin was convinced that the sending of delegates by the remaining counties was not necessarily an expression of popular will. "Ten of the 34 Counties [*sic*]," he exaggerated, "sent no Delegates . . . in many others the Committees consisting of 10 or 12 Men took upon themselves to name them and the rest . . . were chosen according to the best of my information by one twentieth part of the people."[37] There is nothing in the records to contradict the governor's contention regarding the manner in which the delegates were selected, and it may have been true. In any case, none of the delegates had a *legal* right to represent their counties, a fact emphasized by Martin in his proclamation. But apparently all who were chosen attended the congress, which convened at New Bern on April 3.

Martin at once issued a second proclamation forbidding the delegates to continue meeting, but to no avail. Then, on the next day, the legal assembly of the province convened in the same place. Forty-nine delegates attended the assembly, but forty-eight of these were also members of the provincial congress, which had a membership of sixty-eight. The assembly was thus composed almost entirely of members of the illegal congress. John Harvey was chosen moderator of the congress and speaker of the assembly, and during the ensuing proceedings he served in both capacities. Governor Martin opened the assembly session with a speech condemning the congress and calling upon the delegates to oppose it, but, far from complying with his wishes, on the next day they invited that body to join them, and the two groups were now united into a single convention, though from time to time thereafter they acted in their separate capacities.[38]

That evening Martin sought his council's advice as to whether or not he should dissolve the assembly. He believed his duty as a crown official demanded the dissolution of the assembly since it had "so involved itself in the Body of an illegal convention" that it could not be considered "a separate Body or acting as a Branch of the Constitutional Legislature." But the council demurred. Despite the participation of the members of the assembly in the congress, the council argued, the assembly, as a separate body, had done nothing offensive, and therefore the governor should allow it to sit "until it should offend in its own Name and Character."[39] In this advice the governor reluctantly acquiesced.

The next day the assembly passed a series of resolutions in answer to the governor's address of April 4. The lawmakers insisted that the assembly had the "highest sense of the allegiance due to the king" and did not need to be reminded of it. However, it was the "undoubted right" of the people to petition for a redress of grievances "either in a separate or collective capacity" and therefore necessary for the representatives of the people to meet together in order to agree upon such a petition. Furthermore, "while they conduct themselves in a peaceful and orderly manner they deserve not to be called an illegal meeting, or to have the imputation of sedition cast upon them." The assembly, indeed, refused to deem the congress illegal or to "conceive it derogatory to the power and authority of the Assembly." Whatever steps the people had taken "resulted from a full conviction that the Parliament . . . had, by a variety of oppressive and unconstitutional proceedings made the measures they pursued absolutely necessary." Finally, the assembly expressed "the highest compassion for the sufferings of the Town of Boston" and proclaimed the "fixed and determined resolution" of North Carolinians to act in concert with the people of the other colonies "in every effort to maintain those rights and liberties which as Subjects of a British King they possess."[40]

Meanwhile, the delegates, acting as the provincial congress, proceeded to business. On April 5 they expressed thanks and appreciation to Hooper, Hewes, and Caswell for their work as delegates to the Continental Congress. They appointed all three to serve in the Second Continental Congress and granted them complete freedom of action. All measures they took as delegates were to be "obligatory in honor upon every Inhabitant" in the colony. On the same day the congress approved the Association adopted by the First Continental Congress, and all of the delegates but one, Thomas McKnight, a wealthy merchant of Currituck County, signed it. McKnight was again given an opportunity to sign on April 7, but he refused. Thereupon the congress issued a proclamation accusing him of intentions that were "inimical to American Liberty" and recommending that he be held up "as a proper object of Contempt to this Continent." "Every person" should "break off all connection, and have no further Commercial Intercourse or Dealings with him." As its final act, the congress, in accordance with the provisions of the Continental Association, resolved that arts, manufactures, and agriculture should be encouraged in North Carolina and agreed to urge the counties to offer premiums for the increased production of goods.[41]

The congress adjourned on April 7, but the assembly—the last ever to meet in North Carolina under the crown—remained in session until the next day. In his address to that body of April 4, Martin had asked that it devote serious attention to the exceedingly poor financial condition of the colony, that it establish permanent courts and provide salaries for the judges, and that it appropriate funds for the maintenance of Fort Johnston, located off the Cape Fear. The assembly refused each of these requests and so informed Martin in an impudent address that it drew up and approved on April 7. The address enraged Martin, and the next day he dissolved the assembly.[42]

Before disbanding, the assembly arranged to have its address printed on handbills and distributed throughout the colony. Moreover, it prefaced the address with a claim that Martin had ordered the dissolution before it had had an opportunity to present the address to him, and thus it sought to demonstrate that he had acted against it without adequate grounds. But the governor's grounds were substantial. Not only had the assembly refused to take action on every official matter brought before it, but it had eagerly given its approval to every measure taken by the illegal congress.[43] Even so, to dissolve the assembly was a useless and empty gesture at this time. The tide of radicalism had risen too high for such a measure to have any effect other than to increase revolutionary agitation. Every move that the governor made from this point on was seized upon by the radicals and turned to their own advantage. Martin's authority was gone, and he knew it. "I am bound in conscience and duty," he wrote to the Earl of Dartmouth, secretary of state for the colonies, to admit "that Government is here as absolutely prostrate as impotent, and that nothing but the shadow of it is left." With unwarranted optimism, however, he hoped that the future would bring a change for the better.[44]

III

Committees, Congresses, and Councils: The Seizure of Power

Just eleven days after Governor Martin dissolved the General Assembly, patriots in arms clashed violently with British troops at Lexington and Concord in Massachusetts, and the Revolutionary War began. News of these alarming events reached New Bern on May 3 and within a week had swept the province. In the same month reports, which proved to be true, began to circulate that Martin was seeking to secure professions of loyalty from people throughout the colony and that he intended to call to arms a large force of people believed to be staunchly loyal in the interior counties—notably the Scots Highlanders of the upper Cape Fear region and the former regulators and their supporters in the backcountry—in an effort to stamp out sedition and restore royal authority.[1] So wary of Martin's intentions had the patriots of New Bern become by May 23, in fact, that when he dismantled some cannon in the palace yard that morning a "motly mob," led by Abner Nash of the local committee, marched upon the palace and demanded that he remount them. Protesting that he had dismounted the cannon to have them repaired, Martin succeeded in placating Nash and his compatriots, but the incident, occurring in the midst of rising agitation in the coastal area, filled the governor with apprehension for his safety and that of his family. Accordingly, he dispatched his wife and children aboard a ship for New York and fled New Bern to seek the protection of British arms at Fort Johnston at the mouth of the Cape Fear River where he arrived safely, a bitter and discouraged—but not yet defeated—man.[2] For within the confines of the fort he proceeded with plans for reestablishing by force of arms the king's government over North Carolina.

The news from Massachusetts together with the rumors of Martin's efforts to curry loyalist support increased patriot solidarity in the spring of 1775, particularly in the eastern counties, and greatly intensified the vigilance and ardor of the committees and patriot leaders. On May 31 the committee for New Bern and Craven County, headed by Richard Cogdell, denounced the British march on Lexington and Concord as a "most bloody and barbarous Action" against the inhabitants, whom the redcoats "unmercifully fell upon and murdered in cool Blood, and without Provocation . . . having no Regard to Age, Sex, or Infirmity; at the same Time ravaging the Country, burning, destroying, and laying all waste wherever they came. . . ." This description, grossly exaggerating British misdeeds and designed to inspire patriot cohesiveness and hostility, prefaced a local version of the Association that the committee called upon the people of New Bern and Craven County to sign. The Association professed the loyalty of the people to the king, pledged their determination to defend him against the "wicked Ministry," denounced the Coercive Acts as violations of America's "most valuable Liberties," and asserted that these liberties could be preserved only through "a firm Union of the Inhabitants." Shocked at the "cruel" events in Massachusetts and "determined never to become Slaves," the document continued,

> We do hereby agree and associate, under all the Ties of Religion, Honour, and Regard for Posterity, that we will adopt and endeavour to execute, the Measures which the General Congress, now sitting at Philadelphia, may conclude on, for preserving our Constitution, and opposing the Execution of the several arbitrary and illegal Acts of . . . Parliament; and that we will readily observe the Directions of our General Committee for the Purposes aforesaid, the Preservation of Peace and good Order, and Security of Individuals and private Property.[3]

The Association was thus not only a pledge of resistance to Parliament, but a kind of temporary civil compact in which the people who signed it agreed to invest the Continental Congress, the general committee of correspondence of the province, and, by implication, the local committee with the authority of government. This authority the New Bern committee had in fact already assumed, and it now exerted itself to secure the general acceptance of the Association. On June 18 Cogdell reported that in Craven County the document had already been "Generally Signed." Little wonder, for all who refused were immediately branded with the stigma of disloyalty: "Enemies to their Country," they were called.[4]

The New Bern committee not only worked energetically to rally local support, but it also took the lead in promoting resistance throughout the province. It sent out a circular letter to all of the counties and towns in the colony, which was accompanied by copies of the New Bern Association and the "Proceedings" of the committee for May 31. The latter recommended that the people of the town and county form military companies and nominate "proper Officers," named fourteen leading citizens to "summon together the several Companies," and urged the companies to meet twice a month "to advise and consult together how they may best act with united Force, in Case of any sudden and dangerous Emergency." The circular letter called attention to Martin's efforts to recruit loyalist support and recommended to all of the towns and counties that they adopt measures similar to those taken by the New Bern committee in order to provide for "our common Safety and Defence."[5]

On the same day that the New Bern committee adopted its Association and drafted its circular letter to the counties and towns, May 31, a far more radical committee, led by Thomas Polk, met at Charlotte in Mecklenburg County and drew up a series of unusually bold resolves. The resolves denied the authority of Parliament over the colonies and, for the present, that of the king as well: "we conceive that all Laws and Commissions confirmed by, or derived from the authority of the King or Parliament, are annulled and vacated, and the former civil Constitution of these Colonies for the present wholly suspended." Therefore, "the Provincial Congress of each Province, under the Direction of the Great Continental Congress, is invested with all legislative and executive Powers . . . and . . . no other Legislative or Executive does or can exist, at this Time, in any of these Colonies." Since, in the committee's view, all former laws were suspended, and since a provincial congress had not yet enacted new ones, it was necessary for the committee to establish regulations of government for the county, and it proceeded to do so. The inhabitants must form nine military companies and select a colonel and lesser officers. Each company must choose two "Selectmen" empowered to settle all minor controversies involving debts within the company, their decisions to be subject to appeal to a board of selectmen of the entire county. Every selectman was empowered to examine and commit to confinement persons accused of petty larceny, and in each company the two selectmen were to choose two constables to aid them in the execution of their office. The eighteen selectmen were to meet quarterly as a board to hear all disputes involving amounts over forty shillings and all appeals. In felony cases the selectmen could commit convicted persons to close confinement until the provincial congress established a mode of procedure. Quitrents and taxes were to be turned over to the committee of safety, which would disperse the money as "public Exigencies may require." Anyone who received or attempted to exercise a commission from the crown was to be deemed an "Enemy to his Country" and be subject to arrest and confinement. Anyone refusing to obey the resolves would be deemed "equally criminal" and subject to the same punishment. The resolves would remain in force until the provincial congress directed other-

The Mecklenburg Resolves of May 31, 1775, as reported by the *North Carolina Gazette*, June 16, 1775.

wise, or until Parliament gave up "its unjust and arbitrary Pretensions with respect to America." The county's militia companies were to arm and remain constantly ready to execute the orders of the provincial congress or the local committee.[6]

The daring nature of the Mecklenburg Resolves created widespread excitement and doubtless served to embolden the patriots in other areas of the province. They were published in full in the *North Carolina Gazette* of June 16 and thus received wide circulation, for newspapers containing news of revolutionary activities were passed from hand to hand and sent from committee to committee throughout the colony. Radical leaders on the seaboard were both pleased and surprised at the resolves. Richard Cogdell dispatched a copy of the *Gazette* to Caswell at Philadelphia. "You'l Observe the Mecklinburg [sic] Resolves exceed all other committees," he wrote, "or the Congress itself." Samuel Johnston thought the Mecklenburgers' posture may have been even too advanced. "Tom Polk . . . is raising a very pretty spirit in the back Country," he wrote to Joseph Hewes, "he has gone a little farther than I would chose [sic] to have gone but perhaps no further than was necessary. . . ."[7]

To the reports of Martin's activities among the regulators and Scots and the news of Lexington and Concord were now added rumors that struck real fear into the colony's citizens and probably made patriots of many who hitherto had wavered—rumors that Governor Martin intended to free the slaves and set them against the patriot population. In its proceedings of May 31, which were circulated throughout the colony, the New Bern committee warned against this possibility: "in these Times of general Tumult and Confusion . . . the Slaves may be instigated and encouraged by our inveterate Enemies to an Insurrection, which in our present defenceless State might have the most dreadful Consequences. . . ." The committee advised, therefore, that detachments of militia be sent out periodically to patrol and search the Negro houses and seize all arms and ammunition found and all Negroes who appeared suspicious.[8]

As spring gave way to summer rumors of a slave revolt increased, fear heightened, and extensive precautions were taken. On June 21 the Wilmington-New Hanover committee established patrols to watch the Negroes and seize any arms found in their possession. Shortly thereafter an observer reported that the whole town of Wilmington was in "an uproar" over the danger of an insurrection. A great number of armed Negroes had been discovered in the woods, had been disarmed, and one had been killed. Every man in the area was in arms and the patrols searched the house of every Negro to see that all were indoors by nine at night.[9]

On July 1, the Pitt County committee appointed 140 patrollers and stipulated that any slave found away from his master's lands without a pass was to be whipped severely and all armed Negroes were to be disarmed. A week later the same committee received news from Beaufort County that an insurrection was scheduled to take place "against the whole people" that night (July 8). The committee immediately resolved that the patrollers might shoot armed Negroes who refused to surrender their arms as well as Negroes gathered in groups of four or more who were away from their masters' plantations and refused to surrender. By night, nearly forty Negroes had been apprehended and confessions drawn from them disclosed "a deep laid Horrid Tragic Plan laid for destroying the inhabitants of this province without respect of persons, age or sex." These and other Negroes taken up during the next week confessed that they had planned to destroy the families where they lived, then move from house to house, burning as they went, till they reached the backcountry, where they were to receive protection from persons "appointed and armed by Government . . . and as a further reward they were to be settled in a free government of their own." The committee harshly punished the Negroes believed to be involved; some were severely whipped while others had their ears cropped.[10]

Though the Negro testimony charged that the conspiracy was officially inspired, it seems unlikely that this was the case. Governor Martin, of course, vigorously denied it, but more important, such a step at this time would have been foolhardy in the extreme. Though Martin was organizing military support in the backcountry with which to restore royal authority, he was by no means ready as yet to take any overt action, and he must have seen that a premature slave revolt would only unify patriot ranks and undermine completely his plans. That he intended to use the slaves against the patriots, however, was widely believed, and the discovery of the Pitt County "plot" must have confirmed this belief in many minds and intensified hostility against the governor and the royal administration.[11]

The view that Martin would take such extreme action was also underscored by the disclosure of definitive proof of his complicity with the loyalists. In the middle of June the New Bern committee obtained a letter to Martin from a friend in New England who commented on the governor's plans for raising up the loyalists, and on July 2 the Charleston, South Carolina, committee seized the mail just in from England and discovered a letter from Dartmouth to the governor approving and encouraging those plans. The contents of this letter the Charleston committee quickly forwarded to the New Bern committee. "You see he means, and is ordered," wrote the Charleston committee, "to arm one part of your people against the other. We trust that you will . . . act with due vigour and policy . . . to defeat so diabolical a

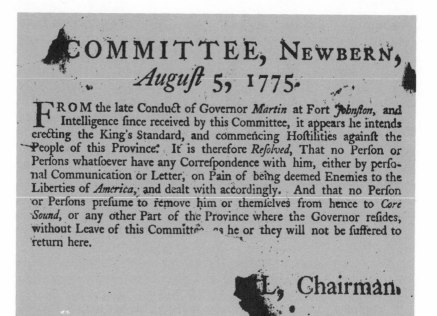

COMMITTEE, NEWBERN,
August 5, 1775.

FROM the late Conduct of Governor *Martin* at Fort *Johnston*, and Intelligence since received by this Committee, it appears he intends erecting the King's Standard, and commencing Hostilities against the People of this Province. It is therefore *Resolved*, That no Person or Persons whatsoever have any Correspondence with him, either by personal Communication or Letter, on Pain of being deemed Enemies to the Liberties of *America*, and dealt with accordingly. And that no Person or Persons presume to remove him or themselves from hence to *Core Sound*, or any other Part of the Province where the Governor resides, without Leave of this Committee as he or they will not be suffered to return here.

L, Chairman.

Richard Cogdell, chairman of the New Bern Committee of Safety, chastised the actions of royal Governor Josiah Martin in this handbill held by the North Carolina State Archives.

design." At about the same time North Carolina's delegates to the Continental Congress learned that Martin had requested a supply of gunpowder from the British army and had sent a cutter to New York to receive it.[12]

To the knowledge that the governor planned to mobilize the loyalists and the fear that he would provoke a slave revolt was added in these anxious weeks rumors that the British intended to set the Indians against the whites along the frontier.[13] Unquestionably, popular apprehension of these dangers was of paramount importance in promoting patriot solidarity and preparedness. Of great importance, also, was the work of individual leaders like Samuel Johnston, Cornelius Harnett, Abner Nash, Richard Cogdell, John Ashe, and Thomas Polk. As leading members of existing committees they exerted themselves during these weeks to promote the formation of revolutionary organizations both political and military in nature and to arouse popular feeling in the counties and towns where little action had yet occurred.[14] The colony's delegates to the Continental Congress, William Hooper, Joseph Hewes, and Richard Caswell, also labored at this time to stimulate revolutionary ardor and military preparedness. They wrote letter after letter to local leaders back home urging them to action, and on June 19 they sent a circular letter to the "People of North Carolina" in which they recounted the long list of British violations of colonial rights and liberties during the preceding decade and implored the citizens to form military companies, preserve their gunpowder, and train themselves in the arts of war. "In one word," they wrote, "The Crisis of America is not at a great distance . . . Everything depends upon your present exertion & prudent perseverence Be in a state of readiness to repel every stroke that . . . must wound and endanger her . . . & consider every man as a traitor to his Sovereign who infringes the rights of his American subjects or attempts invade these glorious Revolution principles which placed our King on the throne [and] must preserve him there."[15]

As report after report and rumor after rumor swept the province, as the committees and individual leaders entered into fervent propaganda and organizational activity, North Carolina was transformed rapidly into a seat of extensive military activity and government by committee. One county after another made military preparations and raised companies during the summer of 1775, and throughout the province the county and town committees grew in size, gained in strength, and increasingly assumed the functions of government. For only a few of the colony's thirty-five counties does the record reveal no sign of revolutionary organization by the end of summer. Many of the committees adopted associations similar to that of the New Bern committee and proceeded to demand the signatures and compliance of the people. While the records of committee activities are incomplete and frequently sketchy and thus do not reveal the formal adoption of the Association in a number of cases, there can be no doubt that the committees generally either formally adopted it or gave their tacit consent.[16]

> Up to this time [1776] most of the inhabitants of the land had associated themselves together against Great Britain [wrote the Moravian, Traugott Bagge], but had had no patience with those who would not join in the Association. But as the latter party did not keep still, but became active for the King in word and deed, the former began to take measures against them. Among other things all arms were forcibly taken from the Non-Associators, and they were compelled to take an oath to remain quiet and not to act against the land.[17]

Actually, enforcement of the Association was one of the most important functions of the committees. Violations included everything that the committees considered injurious to the patriot cause: failing to observe the injunctions of the continental or provincial congresses or the provincial committee or local committees of safety; speaking or writing against any of these bodies or in such a manner as to indicate approval of British policies; selling goods at a price above that set by the committees; exporting goods to the British; fraternizing with non-associators or engaging in trade with them; or refusing to participate in militia activities. In short, a person might be charged with violating the Association for any conduct that the committees deemed "unpatriotic."

During the summer and fall of 1775, dozens of persons were hauled before the committees and charged with violations of the Association. And the committees, sitting as judge and jury, meted out punishments. Thus, in August, 1775, one Anthony Warwick was charged before the Northampton County committee with conveying powder in a "clandestine manner" from Virginia to Hillsborough. He was found guilty of violating the Association in a "flagrant manner" and publicly stigmatized as an "enemy to the rights and liberties of America" who should be "held in the utmost detestation by all lovers of *American* freedom." In a similar case, Captain George Davidson was brought before the Rowan County committee in September and charged with supplying the Cherokees with ammunition, but he was adjudged innocent. The same committee ordered John Perkins to appear before it to "give an account of his political sentiments relative to American Freedom." Perkins gave a satisfactory account of his views, but Jacob Beck, accused of "notorious contempt" of the committee and "opposition to the American measures," refused to recant and was ordered to jail. Later in the day, however, he experienced a change of heart, professed his approbation of the "American measures," and signed the Association. In July, the New Bern committee stigmatized the Reverend James Reed, Anglican clergyman of that town, because he refused to conduct a religious service on June 20, which had been designated by the Continental Congress as a day of "fasting, humiliation and prayer" in honor of the patriots of Boston. The vestry of the parish suspended him from his ministerial office and his salary as well. In August the same committee deemed all who had not signed the Association enemies of their country and ordered that they be dispossessed of all arms and ammunition, which were to be distributed among the patriots. At Wilmington the work of enforcing the Association was undertaken with vigor. According to Governor Martin, John Ashe, with a band of four or five hundred men, went about the town threatening those who refused to sign the document with military execution unless they did so at once. "His cowardly intimidations of these individuals," complained the gov-

This London mezzotint of the Sons of Liberty at Williamsburg, dated February 16, 1775, depicts the patriots as ruffians forcing loyalists to sign the Association. The statue in the background is Lord Botetourt, the former royal governor of Virginia. The tobacco barrel is a present to John Wilkes, mayor of London, arch-opponent of Parliament, and friend to the American cause. From *The Revolution in Drawings and Prints,* 280.

ernor, "so far answered his purpose that they were obliged to sign. . . ."[18]

Though the record does not reveal that nonassociators were executed anywhere in the province, they were sometimes jailed until they recanted and agreed to sign, and frequently they were publicly denounced by the committees. On occasion physical violence was employed against them, sometimes apparently with the knowledge and approbation of the committees, at other times simply by bands of zealous or drunken patriots. Even men of patriot sentiment were sometimes shocked at the excesses committed by their more violent brethren. "The times here begin to be very troublesome," wrote Robert Smith from Edenton toward the end of May, "they Tarr'd & feathered two poor Devils last week and set them Over to Tryell, this week they threaten to serve all my Country men [the Scottish] the same way." A notorious case that occurred in the same town and involved Cullen Pollok, a suspected tory, horrified some of the local revolutionary leaders. Charged with making an unpatriotic remark, Pollok was taken up and kept under guard overnight on orders from the Edenton committee, but the next morning he explained his conduct to the committee's satisfaction and was dismissed. Unfortunately, however, he had made some disrespectful remarks about certain militia officers, who then gathered a number of soldiers "and such Scoundrels as they could prevail with to join," invaded his house at 4 A.M., roused him from bed, and marched him to the courthouse where they tarred and feathered him. Returning to Pollok's house, they drank his stock of liquor and

47

extorted money from him. His wife, meanwhile, scarcely able to bear the torture to her husband, went nearly wild with dread and anguish and finally fainted dead away. Amid rumors that the Pollok's house would be torn down by the mob, some patriot leaders manifested their distress over the affair and condemned it, including Samuel Johnston, who gave the Polloks shelter and protection at his home.[19]

Reports from other counties reveal that violence and harsh treatment of suspected opponents of the Revolution were by no means restricted to the seaboard. In October it was reported from Halifax that no one dared to speak "the least disrespectful" of the provincial congress, "or Tar & Feathers are his Portion," and further west in Surry County many men who had "too plainly expressed their attachment to the British Government" were "run down and" injured "in person, reputation and property." A particularly reprehensible case involved certain zealous patriots of Rowan, Mecklenburg, and Tryon counties, on the western fringe of the province. They actually took up and spirited away to South Carolina two tory attorneys of Rowan County, Benjamin Boote and John Dunn, who had signed a document pledging their allegiance to crown and Parliament and denouncing the Boston patriots for their resistance to British measures. They were also rumored to be organizing resistance to the revolutionary movement in the backcountry. Brought before the South Carolina provincial congress at Camden, they were remanded by that body to Charleston, where, according to Dunn, they were offered their freedom if they would absolve everyone involved in the affair of responsibility, but this they refused to do. In consequence, they were kept prisoners for more than a year without having been tried or convicted of any offence.[20]

The foregoing cases underline the fact that a general breakdown of law occurred in North Carolina as the committees replaced the county courts as the agencies of local government. In countless cases suspected loyalists had their property searched and sometimes seized. They were embarrassed, coerced, and jailed. They suffered cruel punishments without regard for common law guarantees that the patriots accused the crown of subverting. In many cases the perpetrators of the mistreatment—sometimes without even the authority of the committees to support them—went untried and unpunished.

The tory question apart, there was also a general rise of robbery and vandalism in the province. "On account of the present condition of things, the laws are not being enforced, and so theft and robbery are frequent," wrote one observer in September, 1775. The problem of people absconding from their communities without paying their debts also became serious in these months. Though the committees were primarily concerned with matters of defense and propaganda, they assumed, with varying success, the legal and law enforcement functions of the former justices and sheriffs and acted as courts for the settlement of local disputes. Indeed, problems involving private indebtedness, formerly dealt with by the county courts, became one of the most important civil concerns of the committees. The Bute County committee, for example, passed a resolve in November that debtors must give security to their creditors. If a debtor refused, the committee was to cause his person or effects, "at the option of the Creditors, to be seized" until the security was forthcoming or the creditors otherwise satisfied. In numerous cases the committees gave leave to creditors to bring suit for debt, and sometimes the committees prescribed punishments, including incarceration in jail, for debtors who did not fulfill their obligations. The committees also assumed the functions of the county courts in collecting back taxes, in regulating prices, and in calling and conducting elections.[21]

It became apparent, however, as law and order broke down in the province and the threat from Britain loomed more ominous, that government by local committee alone was by no means adequate to meet the multifarious problems of the time. More effective revolutionary and governmental organization—and especially a central executive authority that could coordinate and direct the activities of the committees—was essential. Such could be established only through a Third Provincial Congress, which the patriot leaders now proceeded to call.

The congress convened on August 20, 1775, at Hillsborough. Elections had been held in every county of the province and in nine towns, and 214 delegates were returned, but the record shows that only 184 ever appeared. Still, this was a goodly gathering, far larger than had attended either of the previous congresses. The counties had been encouraged to return larger delegations than in the past, undoubtedly to involve greater numbers of local leaders in the revolutionary movement and thus strengthen support for it. Present were the colony's principal patriot leaders, many of whom were men of substantial ability and long experience in colonial government. Others, little known except perhaps in their home counties, were to make their marks during the Revolutionary period. Samuel Johnston was elected president.

During its first week the congress organized and occupied itself with measures designed to bolster support for the cause in the province, especially among groups considered cool or antipathetic to the Revolution, notably the Moravians, the former regulators, and the Scots Highlanders. Committees were appointed to confer with these groups and to induce them "by Argument and Persuasion, heartily to unite with us for the protection of the Constitutional rights and privileges" of America. The former regulators were to be assured that the crown could no longer impose punishment upon any of them and that the congress would do its utmost to see that they were "protected from every attempt to punish them by any Means whatever"—an assurance designed to squelch rumors that the regulators were still liable to punishment and would be pardoned only if, when called, they took up arms against the patriots. The congress also appointed a committee to draft an "Address to the Inhabitants" in which the controversy with Britain was to be explained in an "easy familiar stile . . . obvious to the very meanest Capacity, calling on them to unite in defence of American liberty, and vindicating . . . the taking up Arms . . . ." In September the congress adopted unanimously an "Address to the Inhabitants of the British Empire," which sought to justify the colony's participation in the revolutionary movement. Reflecting the moderate character of the congress, the address emphatically denied that independence was the objective of the province, affirmed North Carolina's loyalty to the crown, and explained that its only object was to be restored with the other colonies to their status prior to 1763.[22] Though the congress soon took steps to establish a provisional government in North Carolina and to make preparations for defense, hope remained strong among the delegates that some means of reconciliation with Britain might still be found.

On August 23 the congress adopted the Association of the Continental Congress and a "Test" that was to be administered to all members of the provincial congress and all public officials in the colony. The "Test" expressed allegiance to the king and acknowledged his "constitutional executive power" but denied categorically the authority of Parliament either to tax or "regulate the internal police" of the colonies and urged resistance "to the utmost" against any parliamentary attempts to exercise such powers. The people were bound, instead, by the acts and resolutions of the continental and provincial congresses, "because in both they are freely represented by persons chosen by themselves." All members of the congress signed the "Test," and in ensuing weeks it was administered to local officials and in many cases substituted by the county committees for the associations they had earlier adopted. The congress also heard cases involving violations of the Association. Several suspected offenders were summoned to explain their conduct, and in every case they admitted having violated the Association, expressed sorrow at having done so, and agreed to abide by it scrupulously in the future.[23] These sudden conversions were no doubt the product of fear rather than of newfound conviction in the justice of the revolutionary cause.

During early September the congress adopted plans for defense and for the establishment of a provisional government for the province— the two major issues that confronted it. Having passed a measure on August 31 for the raising of 1,000 regular Continental troops in North Carolina, on the next day it provided for their division into two regiments of 500 men each, appointed regimental commanders and subordinate officers, and determined to station 400 of the troops in the Wilmington District and 200 each in the Edenton, New Bern and Salisbury districts. Thus, 800 regulars were to be located in the coastal areas, while 200 were to be stationed in the west, probably as a precaution against Indian attacks. A week later the congress passed resolutions providing for the embodiment of 3,000 minutemen. A "Battalion" of 500 minutemen was to be raised in each of the six military districts. They were to be maintained as separate units from the existing militia regiments.[24]

The congress also took measures to secure arms and ammunition and to encourage the production of commodities that had been secured in the past from England or her West Indian colonies. For example, it appointed a seven-member "Committee of Secrecy" to procure arms and ammunition and offered sizable bounties in provincial currency for the production of gunpowder and the ingredients used in its manufacture, woolen and cotton cards, paper, steel, nails, linen, salt, pig iron, and hollow iron ware. To finance the raising of troops and the procurement of supplies the congress provided for the emission of $125,000 in provincial bills of credit, which was to be sunk by an annual tax of two shillings on every taxable person beginning in 1777 and continuing for nine years, unless the emission "should be sooner sunk." The conduct of provincial financial affairs was placed in the hands of two treasurers, one for the northern half of the province and one for the southern. To these posts the congress appointed Samuel Johnston (northern) and Richard Caswell (southern).[25]

One of the most important functions of the congress was the creation of a provisional civil government. On August 24 it appointed a forty-six member committee, which included some of the leading men in the province, to draft a plan of government. Presented to the congress on September 9, the committee's plan was adopted without change that same day. Though intricate, the plan was neither unique

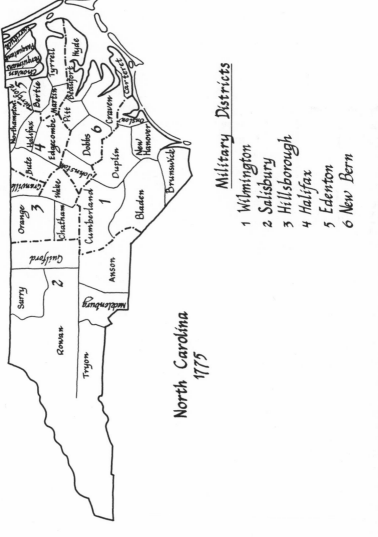

North Carolina
1775

Military Districts

1 Wilmington
2 Salisbury
3 Hillsborough
4 Halifax
5 Edenton
6 New Bern

Map of North Carolina Military Districts, 1775, by Linda Reeves, Division of Archives and History.

nor original. In essence, it was an elaboration and extension of the existing committee system—a natural evolution of the makeshift system of government that had arisen in response to the exigencies of the time. But the plan did clarify and regularize the relationship between the committees, create certain additional committees and define their authority, and establish a much-needed executive authority vested with extensive powers. Indeed, power under this plan was centralized in a small group of men, the provincial council, which was vested with authority over all of the committees and authorized to exercise not merely executive functions, but, under certain conditions, legislative and judicial functions as well.

The provincial council was composed of thirteen members. Each of the six military districts was entitled to two members on the council, as chosen by the congressional delegates of each respective district, while the provincial congress as a whole elected the thirteenth member-at-large. Under the council was a committee of safety in each district, also composed of a president and twelve members. These committees were elected in congress by the delegates from each district. Under the district committees were the county and town committees. In each county there was to be a committee of not less than twenty-one persons, in the towns of Edenton, New Bern, and Wilmington committees of not less than fifteen persons, and in the towns of Bath, Brunswick, Halifax, Hillsborough, Salisbury, and Campbellton, committees of seven persons. All committeemen had to be freeholders, and they were to be elected annually by the freeholders of their respective counties and towns.

The provincial council was vested with the control of all military affairs when the congress was not sitting. The council and the district committees, "in subordination thereto," were to have the "direction, Regulation, Maintenance and Ordering of the Army and of all Military establishments and Arrangements" subject to the ultimate control of the congress, and the council was authorized to draw on the treasury for all necessary sums. Both the council and the district committees were empowered to compel debtors, suspected of planning to leave the colony, to give security to creditors and in default thereof to cause their persons or property to be seized. The district committees, under the "control" of the council, were to "direct the operations of the militia" and other military forces within their jurisdictions, "receive informations & censure & punish delinquents."

The county and town committees were to execute all orders from the council and the district committees and enforce the Association and the resolves and orders of the continental and provincial congresses. They were empowered, as well, to make such further rules and regulations as should be necessary but could "not presume to inflict Corporal punishment on any Offender whatsoever, imprisonment only ex[c]epted . . . ," a restraint designed to prevent the harsh treatment that some of the committees had imposed upon persons in the past. No person was to be permitted to commence an action in any court or before any magistrate without the permission of his local committee. The local committees were also empowered to "take up" and examine suspected persons and send them before the provincial council or the district committees for further examination.

The plan of government also provided for the convening of a provincial congress each year on November 10 at such place as the preceding congress stipulated, though the time and place could be changed by the provincial council. Delegates were to be elected annually in October by the freeholders of each county and the nine towns that were entitled to representation, with each county authorized to return five and each town one. An odd provision permitted householders residing on improved land but without title to it, as well as freeholders, to vote in nine counties located in the heart or on the fringes of the old regulator country, while in the remaining counties only freeholders could vote, an undoubted attempt to woo the former regulators and their sympathizers over to the patriot cause.[26]

The congress thus built upon the existing committee system to create a complex framework of local, district, and provincial government with authority centralized in the provincial council. To this body it elected thirteen men, among them some of the most able and influential in the province, including Samuel Johnston, Cornelius Harnett, Whitmel Hill, Samuel Ashe, Abner Nash, Thomas Person, Willie Jones, and Waightstill Avery. Of the thirteen, seven were lawyers, indicating the significant influence of members of the legal profession in the revolutionary movement in North Carolina, as in the other colonies. At its first meeting, held on October 18, 1775, the council elected Cornelius Harnett president.[27]

During the next six months the members of the council, individually or meeting as a group, devoted much time to the direction of provincial affairs. The threat of a tory rising in conjunction with a possible British invasion by sea necessitated fairly frequent meetings in order that the province might be prepared for defense. The need to implement plans and supervise preparations required that individual members travel to various parts of the province, and even to Virginia and South Carolina. The council met in formal session three times between October, 1775, and March, 1776, though undoubtedly informal meetings between individual members were held on other occasions, and the members kept in close touch with one another by post.

Concerned primarily with defense, the council undertook such varied activities as the acquisition of arms, ammunition, and other supplies, the raising and placing of troops, securing military cooperation from neighboring provinces, and propaganda activities. One of its most difficult problems was that of securing an adequate supply of arms and ammunition. Sufficient quantities could not be acquired in North Carolina or the neighboring provinces, and the council therefore decided to try to import them from abroad. In October it ordered that three vessels be loaded with provisions, each to the value of £1,000, and sent to the foreign West Indies in the hope of exchanging the provisions for arms and ammunition. In December it ordered the dispatch for the same purpose of three or more additional ships with cargoes valued at £500, but this time it did not specify destination. At the same time the council recommended to all friends of freedom in the colony that they purchase all available powder, saltpeter, and sulphur and turn it over to their local committees. It also appointed men in each military district to purchase guns and bayonets and hire gunsmiths. At the end of January, 1776, it purchased 1,000 pounds of gunpowder from South Carolina.

The problem of acquiring arms and ammunition was to become increasingly difficult as time passed, and it was never to be solved, but somehow, through the efforts of the provincial council and the local committees, a sufficient quantity was acquired so that the colony could send reinforcements to both Virginia and South Carolina late in 1775. In the former case nearly a thousand North Carolina men went to the relief of Norfolk, where in December Lord Dunmore deployed a force of tories and Negroes against the patriots, though the Carolinians did not arrive until after Dunmore's defeat; in the latter case nearly a thousand North Carolinians from the western counties cooperated with South Carolina patriots in the defeat of a tory force at Ninety-Six in the so-called "Snow Campaign" of December.

In addition to raising arms, ammunition, and supplies, directing the movement of troops, and concerting cooperative defensive measures with neighboring provinces, the provincial council sought to enforce the Association, provided for the erection of fortifications at vulnerable spots along the coast, arranged for the distribution of propaganda pamphlets in the backcountry, ordered the creation of additional battalions of minutemen and militia, heard cases involving tories and prescribed punishments, and undertook to enforce military discipline and the laws governing the militia and regular troops.[28] All of these activities, of course, were largely the product of the growing fear of a British invasion of the southern provinces by sea in conjunction with a rising of North Carolina's tories.

The latter presently materialized. On January 10, 1776, Governor Martin issued his call to "His Majesty's faithful subjects" to repair to the royal standard, pronounced all who failed to do so "Rebels and Traitors," and authorized loyalist leaders in the western counties to raise loyalist forces, decide upon a place of rendezvous, and march from thence eastward to Brunswick on the coast. Impatient and over-confident of the response, Martin had acted in far too great haste. On February 15, the day the royal standard was raised at the rendezvous point, Cross Creek, the British fleet and army had not as yet arrived off the North Carolina coast. The invasion of the province by British regular forces was an integral part of the plan, and the loyalists counted on it. Its failure to materialize withered loyalist zeal and was of prime importance in discouraging participation in the expedition. The result was that instead of the several thousands Martin expected to rally to the royal cause—undoubtedly a gross overestimation at the outset—only 1,400 men, a motley corps, untrained, inexperienced, poorly equipped and armed, two-thirds of them recently arrived Scots Highlanders, gathered at Cross Creek to make the attempt to wrest the province from patriot control.

The patriot response to the news that Martin had called upon the tories to rise up was immediate. Throughout the province the patriot leaders took precipitous steps to organize resistance, and altogether nearly 10,000 patriot men-in-arms, mostly militia, but including Colonel James Moore's recently organized regiment of Continentals, turned out and prepared to meet the threat. Of these, nearly 2,000 marched against the tories, and about half of that number, under command of Colonel Richard Caswell, intercepted the tory force, now greatly depleted through desertions, at Moore's Creek Bridge some thirty miles above Wilmington and dealt it a devastating defeat. Tory casualties in dead and wounded totaled about seventy, and between twenty and thirty were captured on the scene, while the rest fled the field and scattered. In the wake of the battle, fought on February 27, a general roundup of tories suspected of taking up arms occurred throughout the province. By March 10 some 850 common soldiers had been imprisoned, disarmed, and placed on parole. In addition, over the next two months 125 suspected leaders were tried before a special Committee on Insurgents, and of these, 101 were condemned for conspiracy in the insurrection. Fifty-three were sent out of the province under guard. The twenty-six considered most dangerous were dispatched to Philadelphia, where they were placed under the jurisdiction of the Continental Congress, and the rest to Virginia and Maryland. Though the remainder of the condemned were permitted to remain in North Carolina, they were relocated in counties distant from their homes in order to minimize their influence and ability to create trouble.

The patriot victory at Moore's Creek Bridge frustrated completely the British plan to invade the colony. The unexpectedly great show of patriot strength combined with the defeat and dispersion of the tories led the British expeditionary force, after its belated arrival in March, to leave shortly for the presumably more vulnerable objective of Charleston. Moore's Creek Bridge thus postponed any British attempt to conquer North Carolina until Cornwallis entered the state in September, 1780. More directly, the battle and the problems arising from the tory defeat, as well as the problem of maintaining defenses against a possible British invasion by sea as long as the fleet remained off the southern coast, led the provincial council to issue an immediate call for the convening of the Fourth Provincial Congress.[29]

The congress opened at Halifax on April 4 with only fifty-eight of the 140 elected delegates in attendance, though additional delegates drifted in thereafter until eventually a total of ninety-five appeared— still only about two-thirds of those elected. Samuel Johnston was made president. From the beginning the sessions must have been charged with excitement and apprehension brought on by the belief that despite the tory defeat the province remained in grave danger and that immediate steps must be taken to secure it against invasion. Four British ships of war rode at anchor in the Cape Fear at the time the congress convened, and in ensuing weeks a huge buildup of British naval and military strength occurred as the units of the approaching British fleet under Sir Peter Parker arrived. By mid-May

Sir Peter Parker's fleet led the unsuccessful attack on Charleston in June, 1776. From *The Revolution in Drawings and Prints*, 52.

some seventy British vessels had congregated at the Cape Fear, including seven men-of-war and many large transports carrying several thousand British troops under Generals Clinton and Cornwallis. On May 15 six regiments of these troops landed and encamped at the mouth of the river.[30] The region's patriots must have waited now with anxious minds for this powerful force to strike.

The congress, meanwhile, sought urgently to prepare for this eventuality. During the first few days of its session it appointed committees to deal with various aspects of defense. One was given the task of determining the amount of ammunition in the colony; another was charged with determining further measures "for the better defence of this Province"; a third was given the task of drafting a commission for privateers; a fourth that of estimating the expense of maintaining the troops raised in the province for the period of a year; a fifth was appointed to study methods for "the better regulation of the militia"; a sixth was given the responsibility of determining the best methods of supplying "arms, ammunition, warlike stores and sulphur, and also the expediency of erecting works for the making of salt petre, gunpowder and purifying sulphur"; and a seventh was appointed to serve as a committee of "secrecy, Intelligence and Observation." The last committee, headed by Thomas Burke, was vested with extensive power. It had authority to summon before it all suspected persons, to compel the attendance of witnesses, to subpoena all pertinent documents, and even the power to withhold any information from the congress that might "tend to defeat the purpose of this appointment." The congress also appointed the special committee on insurgents that tried and condemned the tory leaders of conspiracy in the recent insurrection. Burke's committee of secrecy, intelligence and observation, in turn, provided for the disposition of the condemned.[31] Certain of the defense measures taken by the congress were based upon the recommendations of the committees; others resulted from the work of the congress as a whole.

One of the first important acts of the congress was to order an increase in the number of the colony's Continental regiments from two to six and to provide for the raising of three companies of light horse. It proceeded then to adopt an elaborate set of recruiting instructions that detailed the procedures to be used and provided for the payment of a 40 shillings bounty and £3 advance pay to each recruit. It was expected that these troops would be taken into the Continental service and placed on the Continental payroll, and in May the Continental Congress did assume control over the six regiments, though not over the three companies of light horse. The provincial congress also resolved to raise at once five independent companies of sixty-eight rank and file to be stationed at strategic places along the coast, and in May it ordered the drafting of 1,500 militiamen for a term of three months from the Edenton, New Bern, Halifax, and Wilmington districts. These troops, along with an artillery company, also ordered to be raised by the congress, were to be sent to General James Moore on the Cape Fear.[32]

The congress also adopted a new plan of militia organization under which the militia was to be divided into six brigades, one in each of the military districts, with each brigade commanded by a brigadier general. The brigades were to be composed of regiments established in each of the counties and commanded by colonels. The regiments were to be made up of all effective men in each county between the ages of sixteen and sixty.[33]

The problem of raising and organizing military forces was only one that occupied the congress. It was concerned, also, like the provincial council before it, with the concomitant problems of procuring arms, ammunition, and supplies for the troops. To facilitate this important business, it appointed collectors in each county to gather arms and made plans for the establishment of factories to produce saltpeter, gunpowder, salt, iron, and muskets and bayonets. To provide for the cost of these preparations, it voted on May 9 to emit £500,000 in paper bills of credit. These bills were to be redeemed beginning in 1780 by a poll tax which was to continue for twenty years.[34]

Preparations for defense, particularly in the Cape Fear region, presently became less urgent, however, for before the end of the month the British fleet had left North Carolina waters. By June 1 it had anchored off Sullivan's Island in South Carolina, preparatory to the abortive siege of Charleston. The failure of this operation and the return of the British fleet to the north lifted the threat of invasion from the southern states for over two years, during which, except for an uprising of the Cherokees on the western frontier, comparative tranquility reigned.

Meanwhile, the events of the winter and spring of 1776—the tory uprising and the threatened invasion by sea—aroused for the first time support for the idea of the political independence of the colonies from Britain amongst the patriots of North Carolina. Though radical sentiment had been strong in the colony since Lexington and Concord, though the slave insurrection scare that summer and the reports of Martin's machinations with the interior tories intensified that radicalism and cumulatively pushed North Carolinians in the direction of independence, we find no avowed support for that course of ac-

View of Charleston (1768), engraved by C. Canot from an original painting of T. Mellish. From *The Revolution in Drawings and Prints*, 232.

tion amongst the patriot group until the tory rising. From the colony's patriot leaders until that time, indeed, came many expressions of their heartfelt hope that reconciliation might be achieved on "honorable" terms, which meant, of course, a repeal of the Coercive Acts and an agreement that Parliament would not tax the colonies or interfere otherwise in the colonies' internal political affairs. By the time the Fourth Provincial Congress met in early April, however—after Moore's Creek Bridge and as British naval and military strength was building up in the Cape Fear—the position of the patriot leaders had undergone significant change. They had become convinced—albeit reluctantly—that reconciliation on "honorable" terms was beyond reasonable hope.[35] At the Third Provincial Congress, in September, 1775, the delegates, favoring moderate measures that they hoped would preserve the imperial connection with Britain, had rejected a proposed plan of continental confederation, in part, at least, out of fear that formal confederation would widen the breach and make separation inevitable.[36] The radical fourth congress saw no alternative to separation, and on April 12, only five days after it convened, it passed unanimously a resolution by which North Carolina, before any of the other colonies, took an unqualified stand in support of independence:

> Resolved, That the delegates for this Colony in the Continental Congress be impowered to concur with the delegates of the other Colonies in

60

declaring Independency, and forming foreign alliances, reserving to this Colony the sole and exclusive right of forming a Constitution and laws for this Colony, and of appointing delegates from time to time . . . to meet the delegates of the other Colonies for such purposes as shall be hereafter pointed out.[37]

Not only did the congress assert its support of the colonies' declaring their independence from Britain, but it asserted, at the same time, the independence of North Carolina from the other provinces. The new state would draw up its own constitution and laws, establish its own government, and reserve to itself the right of independent action, confederating, for the present at least, only to the extent that it had already done so through the agency of the Continental Congress.

With the giant stride toward independence taken, the congress faced the difficult task of formulating a constitution that would provide for the establishment of a more permanent government. On the very next day, April 13, it appointed a committee for this purpose, which set to work at once.[38] From the beginning of the committee's discussions it was apparent that the question of the nature of the government to be established would become a divisive force in the congress, one that would strain the unanimity that had characterized former congresses and rend this one into factions. Hitherto the issues had been largely those concerning resistance to Britain, the tory

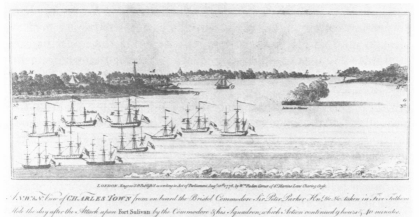

View of Charleston from on board the *Bristol*, taken in Five Fathom Hole the day of the attack on Fort Sullivan; published by William Faden, August 10, 1776. From *The Revolution in Drawings and Prints*, 233.

menace, defense, and the degree to which the province should participate in the common colonial cause, and on these issues there had been substantial agreement. Now arose questions of the organization of government, methods of representation, qualifications for voting and holding office, the nature and powers of the executive, legislative, and judicial branches, the protection of property interests—in short, questions involving the future control of political power in the state.

At the heart of the matter was the question of whether the new government should be conservative, with a legislative body elected by the property owners and reflecting their interests and with appointive executive and judicial officers, or more democratic, with few or no property qualifications for the vote and for holding office and with elective officers and judges. On these issues opposing factions at once arose in the committee, both of which found support in the congress at large. For want of better names these factions have been labeled "conservative" and "democratic," or "radical," by historians of the period. Unfortunately, the paucity of the sources on this question makes it impossible to determine with exactness who composed each group, but in general the support for the more democratic constitution came from the representatives of the western and piedmont counties, while those from the seaboard and eastern counties largely composed the conservative element. The eastern counties had long dominated the colonial government of North Carolina, and there was a long history of sectional controversy between east and west, culminating in the regulator movement of the late 1760s. Westerners had always felt discriminated against by the eastern-controlled government in matters of representation, taxation, and the imposition of legal fines and fees by appointive officials. The regulator movement had sought to correct these inequalities—with little success. Now, in the creation of the revolutionary constitution westerners doubtless saw the opportunity to diminish eastern domination and eradicate the inequalities of the colonial period through greater democracy—specifically through elective instead of appointive judges, clerks, and sheriffs, through a liberal franchise that would insure representation of the small-propertied and unpropertied classes in the legislative body, and through an equitable system of county representation. Contrariwise, the eastern delegates, seeking to control the new government as they had the old and representing the substantial landed interest of the eastern counties, generally supported a conservative system of government patterned more closely to the colonial model.

Apparently the democratic faction, headed by Thomas Burke of

Orange County and Thomas Person of Granville, constituted a majority of the committee and dominated the proceedings, but the conservatives were a strong minority and the two groups could not be reconciled.[39] After a week of nightly meetings, Samuel Johnston, the conservative leader, reported that they had been able to "conclude on nothing."[40] At the end of another week the committee placed recommendations for the new government before the congress, but these did not constitute a detailed and finished constitution. They were merely a series of resolutions setting down the broad outlines of government upon which a majority of the committee had been able to agree. It was anticipated, however, that even these would be altered substantially by the house.

The resolutions provided for a bicameral legislature with a lower house elected by the freeholders and by free householders who had enjoyed that status for at least a year, and an upper house composed of one member from each county for whom only freeholders could vote. All legislation would require the approval of both houses. The executive branch was to be a council composed of a president and six councillors. It would remain in continuous session and conduct the "official business of Government." While these provisions embodying property qualifications for the vote—though a small one for lower-house elections—and providing a check by the upper house on the power of the lower were in harmony with conservative views, the conservatives could not abide the manner in which the executive council was to achieve office—apparently by annual popular election rather than by vote of the legislature.[41]

On the floor of the congress, however, enough dissatisfaction arose over the proposed framework of government to secure its early defeat—to the great relief of conservative committee members like Johnston and William Hooper. Thereupon the congress appointed a new committee to form a temporary government that was to remain in power until the end of the next provincial congress. That congress, the fifth, would function as a constitutional convention and formulate a permanent system of government for the state.[42]

The new committee quickly set to work on the problem of establishing a temporary government but came up with a system little different from that which was in effect. On May 11 the congress adopted a series of resolutions that determined the organization of government during the remainder of 1776. The provincial council was replaced by a new body, identical in structure, but denominated the council of safety. It was composed of thirteen members who were elected in precisely the same manner as their predecessors on the provincial council. The new council of safety was vested with full power "to do and execute all acts and things necessary for the defence and protection of the people of this Colony," but specific limitations were placed upon this power. It could not "alter, suspend, or abrogate" any resolution of the congresses, emit bills of credit, levy taxes, impose import or export duties, draw on the Continental treasury for funds, or "erect any office or offices, courts or jurisdictions, or . . . try, adjudge, or condemn, any person . . . for any offence," save where expressly permitted by resolution of congress. There were, however, significant exceptions to these restrictions. Nothing in the resolutions was to be construed in such manner as to prevent the council of safety from "examining and committing any person . . . who may be accused on oath of practices inimical to America, or to restrain any person . . . from departing . . . by Sea." Moreover, on "any urgent exigency" it could direct the provincial treasurers to draw on the Continental treasury for sums totaling up to £30,000. The district committees of safety were abolished under the new plan of government, and their powers and functions were vested in the council of safety. Thus, the new plan, while similar to the old, provided for a less decentralized system and concentrated even greater authority in the council.

On the same day that the congress adopted the new plan of government it chose the council. Willie Jones of Halifax, one of the wealthiest men in the colony but known to have strong democratic leanings, was the choice of the congress at large. His selection in place of Johnston, who had held the comparable position in the provincial council and had served as president of the two preceding congresses, suggests that Johnston's staunchly conservative, perhaps uncompromising, stand on the constitution had reduced his popularity and temporarily, at least, enhanced the position of the democratic faction. Nor was Johnston elected to the council by the delegates of the Edenton district, though his friend and supporter, Thomas Jones, received a place. Nevertheless, considerable continuity of leadership was maintained between the first provisional government and the second, for eight of the thirteen elected to the council of safety had been members of the provincial council. Other whig leaders who did not receive places on the council of safety were given positions of importance. William Hooper, Joseph Hewes, and John Penn were reelected provincial delegates to the Continental Congress, and Caswell and Johnston were continued as the two provincial treasurers. Before it adjourned on May 14, the congress stipulated that the fifth congress would convene at Halifax on November 10, unless called into session sooner by the council of safety.[43]

During the next six months provincial affairs were in the hands of the council of safety. It functioned in much the same way as its predecessor, the provincial council, and faced many similar problems. An itinerant body, headed in turn by Cornelius Harnett, Samuel Ashe, and Willie Jones, it sat first in one district, then in another, in an effort to keep a close watch on affairs throughout the colony. One of its continuous concerns was the tory problem. Despite the recent tory defeat, the roundup and confinement of tory leaders, and the departure of the British fleet for Charleston, tory activity had not completely ended. Here and there, during these months, minor incidents involving tories occurred, and many individual tories were charged with correspondence with the enemy, rabble-rousing, propaganda activities, or refusing to accept the province's new revolutionary currency. Dozens of such persons were called before the council, tried, and convicted as charged. Some were committed to jail; others were placed on parole under the surveillance of the local committee in places far removed from their homes; some were allowed to remain free in their communities but were required to take the oath and post sizable bonds as guarantees of their future good behavior. The council also inaugurated measures to diminish tory activity by threatening the property of the disaffected with confiscation if they did not mend their ways, and in some cases it actually proceeded to confiscation. Thus began a policy that was to result in the seizure by the revolutionaries of vast amounts of tory property before the Revolution ended.

The tory problem was only one of several that confronted the council. It was equally concerned, like the provincial council before it, with the procurement of military supplies, especially lead, arms, powder, and salt, and in pursuit of this objective it promoted the establishment of iron and salt works, the collection of lead by the state's militia companies, and the exportation of lumber products (staves and shingles) to the West Indies to be exchanged for military items. It also commissioned and sent out privateers in the hope that they might damage British commerce and bring in prizes laden with military supplies.[44]

The concern of the council with the problem of securing military supplies indicates the continuing importance of the problem of defense. Though the British had departed the Cape Fear, the need to continue military preparations seemed imperative, for the council feared that they might return. Moreover, even as the fleet departed, a second serious threat to provincial security was developing, this time in the west—an uprising of the Cherokee Indians. The Cherokee rising, in fact, created the most serious problem that the council of safety had to face.

Beginning in April, 1776, the Cherokees, angered at white encroachments on their lands, apprehensive of eventual domination by the intruders, and urged on by the young men of the tribe who coveted scalps and glory, began hostilities along the frontier. At first there was no organized uprising, merely intermittent attacks by small groups of braves against isolated families on the far frontier of the province, but by mid-July a large-scale Indian rising was under way and threatening older and more settled areas as far to the east as the border of Mecklenburg County. To meet this challenge, the council of safety took vigorous action. It ordered Brigadier General Griffith Rutherford, commander of North Carolina forces in the western district, to embody his troops and, in cooperation with Virginia and South Carolina forces, undertake an expedition against the Cherokee nation. Rutherford carried out these orders with devastating results. During September, with about 2,000 men under his command, he marched against the Middle and Valley settlements of the Cherokees and laid them waste, virtually without opposition. Meanwhile, in early August, South Carolina troops under Major Andrew Williamson attacked and destroyed the Cherokee Lower towns. Altogether, the two forces destroyed some thirty-six Cherokee towns, along with their stores and crops. While the Indians suffered only light manpower losses, they were dispersed and forced to flee, and they faced the prospect of a winter with little food. Most of them fled southward to the Coosawatchee River, which bordered the territory of the upper Creeks. In October a Virginia force of 900 under Colonel William Christian, augmented by about 300 North Carolinians, invaded the territory of the Overhill Cherokees, burned five of their towns, and negotiated a peace settlement which brought an end to the hostilities. By early November, all was quiet along the southern frontier. The campaign against the Cherokees thus quashed a developing Indian uprising of serious proportions at a very critical period, and though small bands of braves made sporadic and isolated attacks against frontier settlers in the years that followed, it discouraged the Cherokees from attempting any large-scale effort against the whites for the duration of the Revolutionary period.[45]

In the midst of the Indian troubles, the settlers on the Watauga and Holston rivers on the other side of the mountains, seeking the protection of the North Carolina government, had drawn up a petition requesting admission into the state as the Washington District. The council of safety approved this petition on August 22 and recommended that the freemen of the district hold an election for delegates to place their proposal before the Fifth Provincial Congress in November. On November 19 the fifth congress admitted the Washington District into the state and seated its three delegates.[46] In doing so, the congress exercised the authority to create and admit to representation new units of local government, a power formerly exercised by the colonial legislature. This, however, was one of the minor actions of the congress. Its principal work was the creation of a constitution for the new state of North Carolina.

IV
The State Constitution

After abandoning efforts to produce an acceptable state constitution, the Fourth Provincial Congress, it will be recalled, had provided that a new congress be held in November, 1776, which was to function also as a constitutional convention. Accordingly, on August 9 the council of safety issued a call for elections to be held throughout the colony on October 15. The council recommended that each county elect five delegates and took pains to stress the importance of the elections by pointing out that the delegates would be responsible not only for making laws, but for framing a constitution that would be in the future "the Corner Stone of all Law" and "according as it is well or ill Ordered . . . tend to promote the happiness or Misery of this State." [1]

Elections were held in all thirty-five of the colony's counties, in the Washington District, and in nine towns. The division between democrats and conservatives in the preceding congress over the nature of the prospective constitution and the failure of the democratic faction to secure a constitution compatible with its views probably heightened controversy and sharpened the competition for congressional seats in some of these elections, but there is little or no evidence of a concerted, well-organized radical movement in the state to prevent the election of conservatives. The elections were not violent in character, as some historians have contended. The elections were contested by dissatisfied voters in Orange, Guilford, and Bertie counties and in the town of Hillsborough. The group that disputed the Hillsborough returns was doubtless identical with the group that protested in Orange County, since that town was the county seat and the site of both elections. But the record does not reveal whether these challenges resulted from partisanship regarding the nature of the prospective state constitution or whether they were simply brought on by local or personal issues. The fifth congress recognized and seated all of the delegates returned in these disputed contests, though after five days, for reasons not explicated in its journal of proceedings, it reversed its position with respect to the Orange County delegates and called for a new election in that county. Held in December, this election returned a slate of five delegates of which only one, John McCabe, had been elected in the former contest, and which included Thomas Burke, a leader of the democratic faction in the fourth congress.

Tradition has it that a riotous and bitter election campaign occurred that October in Chowan County, where, it has been said, the radicals exerted all their efforts to bring about the defeat of Samuel Johnston because of his conservative position on the constitution. But the fact is we know very little about what transpired in that election. No original account of it exists, and we do not even know for certain that Johnston stood for election, though, in view of his previous leadership in the revolutionary congresses, it would be strange if he had not. In any case, he was not returned to the fifth congress, but the paucity of contemporary evidence makes it impossible to determine with certainty the reason why. The evidence that does exist, however, suggests that Johnston's constitutional views were a less important

Bust of Samuel Johnston in the State Capitol, executed by F. W. Ruckstuhl, 1912.

issue at the time than his rather benevolent attitude toward tories. While he was a firm champion of resistance to Britain and vitally concerned about the security of the state, he at the same time opposed violent or oppressive measures against tories, probably opposed the confiscation of their estates, and had sometimes used his influence in behalf of persons accused of toryism. If indeed he ran for election, this, it appears, was the principal reason for his defeat. Moreover, other men of conservative views were returned from Chowan County in this election, including Thomas Jones, Thomas Benbury, and James Blount. If Johnston's defeat represented a great radical victory in Chowan over the constitutional issue, as some historians have contended, it is strange that these conservatives did not suffer defeat as well.

Many men who had had no previous legislative experience were returned to the fifth congress—33 percent of the 183 members were neophytes—but this figure compares favorably with the percentage of men of no experience elected to the previous four revolutionary congresses: 32 percent on the average. The argument, sometimes made, that an unusually large number of new men were returned to the fifth congress due to radical victories, especially in the piedmont and western counties, therefore does not stand up. There were a good many new men, yes, and nearly as many from the eastern counties as from the piedmont and western counties, but whether they were radicals or conservatives with respect to the constitutional issue the record does not show, and, as indicated, there had been a good many new men elected to all of the revolutionary congresses. The return of new members to the fifth congress, therefore, cannot be taken as evidence of widespread radical success in the elections. And the fact is that the vast majority of old members of long standing—men who had held seats not only in the earlier revolutionary congresses but in the colonial assemblies, as well, men of property who represented the conservative point of view—were returned to the fifth congress just as they had been returned to the earlier ones. Joseph Hewes, Cornelius Harnett, Richard Caswell, Allen Jones, Thomas Jones, Thomas Benbury, James Blount, Samuel Ashe, and John Ashe all received seats. William Hooper was elected by both the town of Wilmington and Perquimans County. According to one study, eight men had stood out as the leaders of the assembly—the wielders of the real political power in the colony—in the period from 1771 to 1775. All of them were among the conservatives returned to the fifth congress and listed above, with the exception of John Harvey, who was dead, Robert Howe, who was on military service, and Samuel Johnston. This is not to say that there was not considerable sentiment in favor of a democratic constitution in the state, but there is no evidence that it was well organized or that those who held democratic views met with any great measure of success in the elections. The conservatives apparently were in the majority at the congress and dominated its proceedings from the outset.[2]

The congress convened on November 12 and unanimously elected Richard Caswell, who was anything but a radical, president. The next day it appointed the nucleus of a committee to draft a constitution and bill of rights, to which it added several additional members in the next few days. Altogether, the committee contained twenty-eight members, including, with few exceptions, the state's most prominent political figures. The members were drawn from all areas of the state, with a larger number from the eastern counties than from the piedmont and western counties. Three of the western members represented Mecklenburg County, which had the largest representation on the committee.[3] The reason, perhaps, was that the Mecklenburg delegates had come to the congress with a detailed set of instructions from their constituents calling for the adoption of a democratic constitution. Thus, they had in their hands a partial plan of government drawn along democratic lines, and the exponents of such a system may have used their influence to secure seats for the Mecklenburg members on the committee. A similar set of instructions was drawn up in Orange County, but it is doubtful that these were carried to the congress by the delegates originally returned. They are unmistakably in the handwriting of Thomas Burke, who was returned to the congress by the special election of December 10, which, it will be recalled, resulted in the defeat of four of the five original delegates. It is probable that these instructions were brought to the congress by Burke and his newly elected colleagues, all of whom arrived too late for appointment or service on the committee on the constitution. Indeed, on the day of the second Orange election the constitution passed its first reading before the congress.[4] It is therefore doubtful that the Orange instructions had any influence on the deliberations of the committee.

The inadequacy of evidence makes it impossible to determine the political bias of all of the committee members. It seems clear, however, that Richard Caswell, Allen and Thomas Jones, John and Samuel Ashe, Archibald Maclaine, Joseph Hewes, Cornelius Harnett, and probably Abner Nash were on the conservative side, while Willie Jones, Thomas Person, Griffith Rutherford, the delegates from Mecklenburg—Hezekiah Alexander, Waightstill Avery, and Robert Irwin—and probably William Sharpe, supported the democratic position. So little is known about the other twelve members that one can scarcely speculate about their political views. Eight of them, however, represented eastern counties, and if geography was an important factor in determining the politics of the delegates, probably most were conservatives. It seems apparent, therefore, both on the basis of the above analysis and the nature of the completed constitution, that the conservatives constituted a clear majority of the committee. One leading conservative who doubtless would have been a member had he been present was William Hooper, but Hooper, though returned by two different constituencies, reluctantly remained in Philadelphia because of the pressing business before the Continental Congress. He made the weight of his opinion felt, however, by sending to the congress a long letter in which he expounded his views regarding the kind of government that ought to be established.[5]

A variety of other influences also came to bear upon the committee. In addition to the Mecklenburg County instructions, possibly the Orange County instructions, and the Hooper letter, a long exposition by John Adams entitled "Thoughts on Government" and the new constitutions of several of the other states were consulted by the committee. Even more influential were the colonial and revolutionary experience of government and, at least indirectly, the natural rights, compact theory as expounded by John Locke, with which colonial politicians in general were so familiar.

The instructions from Mecklenburg and Orange counties are interesting as examples of the democratic position in the state. There were many similarities between the two, though those from Mecklenburg were far more detailed. They called for the establishment of a "simple Democracy or as near it as possible" and ordered the delegates to "oppose everything that leans to aristocracy or power in the hands of the rich and chief men exercised to the oppression of the poor." They further demanded that the delegates work for the inclusion in the constitution of a "bill of rights . . . which shall never be infringed . . . by the law making power or other derived powers in the State." The Orange instructions, though not calling specifically for a bill of rights, contained a provision requiring that the law-making power be so limited by the constitution that it could not alter the "distribution of power" or deprive "any individual of his civil or natural rights unless adjudged against him by the judging power."

Regarding the theory on which government should rest and the particulars of governmental structure, the two sets of instructions had many similarities. Both asserted that there are two kinds of political power, "one principal and superior, the other derived and inferior." The principal or superior power belongs to the people, the derived or inferior power to the "servants which they employ," that is, to any who are "delegated, chosen, employed and trusted by the people." The fundamental document of government, from which the inferior power (the government) derives its power, is the creation of the superior power (the people) and can be altered, suspended, or abrogated only by the superior power, and the authority of the inferior power is limited by that fundamental document. Both sets of instructions called for the new constitution to be submitted to the people for their approval before it went into effect. Thus, the democratic principle of government by consent based upon a fundamental law formulated by the people and binding on a government of their creation was explicit in these instructions.

Both sets of instructions stipulated also that the government should have three separate and distinct branches—executive, legislative, and judicial—and both called for a bicameral legislature with both houses to be elective. The Mecklenburg instructions prescribed only that the two houses should be elected annually "by the people," with all voters having the right to vote for the assembly having also the right to vote for the council. The Orange instructions, on the other hand, prescribed that the lower house should be elected by freeholders and householders, the upper house by freeholders only. On their face, the Orange instructions were the more radical regarding the manner of electing the governor. They provided only that he be elected, and that no person serve more than three consecutive terms or be returned to office in less than three years after serving his third consecutive term. The implication was that the governor should be elected by the voters rather than by the legislative body, though this was not made explicit. The Mecklenburg instructions provided specifically that the governor be elected annually by the legislature in joint session.

Regarding religious practice and the relationship between church and state both sets were explicit. They called for the disestablishment of the Anglican church: no person should be compelled to pay a tax in support of the clergy of any denomination to which he did not belong. The Orange instructions, however, were somewhat more liberal. They demanded complete freedom and toleration for all sects, except that officeholders must "give assurances that they do not acknowledge supremacy ecclesiastical or civil in any foreign power or spiritual infallibility or authority to grant the Divine Pardon to any person who may violate moral duties or commit crimes injurious to the community. . . ." The Mecklenburg instructions called for complete freedom of worship for all "professing Christians," with the exception of "idolatrous worshipers," and no Roman Catholic, atheist, or nontrinitarian should hold public office.

The Orange instructions made no further stipulations about the constitution of government, but those of Mecklenburg prescribed the method by which certain officials should attain office. All delegates to the Continental Congress, all treasurers and secretaries for the state, and the judges of the equity, appeals, and superior courts should be appointed by the General Assembly. They also stipulated that no officer of the regular troops, collector of public monies, or former collector in arrears to the state should be eligible for a seat in the assembly. Finally, they prescribed that "Trials by Jury" should be "forever had and used in their utmost purity."

The Mecklenburg instructions also included a series of proposals for legislation that its delegates should strive to get enacted once the new government was established. Many of these proposals were democratic in nature, reflecting the discontent of the western counties over the inequalities suffered at the hands of the eastern-dominated government during the colonial period, and were reminiscent of the regulator demands of 1770-1771. Included were proposals that all vestry laws and marriage acts be abolished, that a law be passed to "prevent clandestine marriages," and that all "Gospel ministers regularly ordained, whether by Bishops, by Presbyteries or by Association of regular ministers" be granted the legal right to perform the marriage ceremony. Several of the requested measures had as their aim the protection of the poor. One called for an "appraisement law for the relief of the poor when their goods are sold by execution"; another for the annual election in each county of overseers vested with power to provide for the poor. Several were designed to cure or curb the inequalities and injustices that had been perpetrated on the people by "courthouse rings" and corrupt officials in the past. One instructed the delegates to seek a law diminishing the fees of the clerks of courts and clarifying the fee bill so as to eliminate its ambiguities; another instructed them to secure a law providing for the payment by the state of county court justices, thus eliminating the collection of fees by the justices. A third called for tax collectors to be chosen annually in each county (instead of entrusting this job to appointed and permanent collectors); a fourth urged passage of a general and equitable tax on land by which the "people shall be taxed according to their estates" (instead of by poll); and a fifth called for legislation providing that the sheriffs, clerks, and registers of each county annually be elected by the freeholders instead of being appointed. The instructions also called for laws immediately establishing and opening superior and inferior courts, including a court of equity, and for legislation retaining "so much of the *Habeas Corpus* Act and the Common and Statute law" as was "favorable to the liberties of the people . . . excluding every idea of the kingly office and power." [6]

More in harmony with the nature of the completed constitution than the democratic provisions of these county instructions were the conservative views of Hooper and John Adams. Hooper was a firm believer in mixed government, which he believed had been developed to perfection in the historic British constitution (that which was "at present stiled the British Constitution," he wrote, was "an apostate"). This constitution united "the three grand qualities of virtue, wisdom and power as the characteristicks of perfect Government." From the people came virtue; wisdom resided in "a selected few whom superiour Talents or better opportunities . . . had raised to a second class"; power rested in the hands of someone "whom variety of Circumstances may have placed in a singular and conspicuous point of view, and to whom Heaven had given talents to make him the choice of the people to entrust with powers for sudden and decisive execution." Hooper here expounded the so-called "classical theory" of the British constitution, according to which the qualities he mentioned were represented in the British government, in reverse order, by king, lords, and commons. They combined in admirable fashion the three characteristics that such classical scholars as Aristotle and Polybius had held were essential—in proper balance—to perfect government: monarchy, aristocracy, and democracy.

In the present British government, of course, the three qualities had become dangerously out of balance in Hooper's view. The powers of the crown had become too independent of the people. These powers had been derived from the people and were "subject to Revocation," but in Britain the kingly power had been long exercised over an "inattentive people" and had thus assumed "the appearance of being the inherent right of sovereignty." It was necessary, therefore, that under such a system "recurrence should often be had to original principles to prevent" that evil from occurring.

Could not these historic principles of mixed government in their "pure, genuine, unadulterated" form be the basis of the new constitution of North Carolina? Hooper thought so. The new system of government need change but little from the old, for the people of the state had long been used to a system of mixed government. And since the end of all government is the happiness of society, this end can best be promoted by "assimilating it to the tempers, pursuits, customs & Inclinations of those who are to be ruled." He hoped, therefore, that in framing the new constitution "much regard" would be paid to "the prevalence of habit, & that system adopted which will remedy the defects of the policy under which we have lately lived, without such a violent deviation as may tend to produce a convulsion from unnecessary alterations."

The historic British constitution, with its admirable blending of virtue, wisdom, and power, should serve then as the principal model for the constitution of North Carolina. The legislative body should be bicameral, with a lower house representing the people and an upper house composed of members of that second class which talent, experience, and property had elevated above the rest. The upper house might well, indeed, be "a refinement of the first choice of the people at large, selected for their Wisdom, remarkable Integrity, or that

William Hooper, one of North Carolina's signers of the Declaration of Independence, offered the Halifax Congress his own thoughts on what the new state constitution should contain. Engraving by E. G. Williams and Brothers, from Samuel A. Ashe (ed.), *Biographical History of North Carolina* (Greensboro: Charles L. Van Noppen, 8 vols., 1905-1917), VII, facing p. 233.

weight which arises from property and gives Independence and Impartiality to the human mind." A unicameral legislature Hooper considered entirely unacceptable. Such a legislature was "a many headed Monster which without any check must soon defeat the very purposes for which it was created, and its members become a Tyranny dreadful in proportion to the numbers which compose it." The first revolutionary constitution of Pennsylvania, which provided for a single house, was an example of the complete inadequacy of such a system. There, fortunately, the "people soon saw the Monster the Convention had framed . . . with horror, and with one accord stifled it in its cradle. . . ." Hooper indicated that he once thought an executive veto on acts of legislation desirable, but he had now concluded that such was unnecessary, for power of that sort in the hands of an individual is liable to abuse, and besides it was unreasonable "that an individual should abrogate at pleasure the acts of the Representatives of the people, refined by a second body whom we may call for fashion's sake Counsellors. . . ." But the constitution should nevertheless provide for a "Magistrate solely executive" who, with the aid of a council, should have "such executive powers as may give energy to Government."

At this same time Hooper sent to the congress the new constitutions of several states with comments concerning their merits. The constitution of Delaware he thought excellent. It differed little from the old proprietary charter of government, "abolishing little else but the regal and proprietary powers and deriving all powers from the people." No part of it did he admire more than "the appointing Judges

76

This portrait of John Adams was painted by Charles Willson Peale about 1794 while Adams was vice-president of the United States. It is on permanent loan to the Independence National Historical Park in Philadelphia. For a complete history of the portrait, see Andrew Oliver, *Portraits of John and Abigail Adams* (Cambridge, Mass.: Harvard University Press, 1967), 70-72.

during good behaviour." If judges were made elective officials and their terms of office limited, "that instant you corrupt the Channels of public Justice." From the Delaware constitution and those of New Jersey and South Carolina, Hooper believed, a system of government might be framed "that may make North Carolina happy to endless ages." Those of Pennsylvania and Rhode Island, however, with their "monstrous" radical provisions, should be avoided like the plague.[7]

The important essay by John Adams, "Thoughts on Government," originally written in the form of a letter sent to William Hooper and John Penn after they had asked Adams to express his views on the subject, and later published in a slightly altered version in pamphlet form (April, 1776), was apparently widely consulted by the political leaders of the day and probably had an influence on several of the new state constitutions, including that of North Carolina.[8] In this essay Adams expressed the view that the happiness of the people is the end of government and that that government is best "which will produce the greatest quantity of happiness." And since the happiness of mankind "consists in virtue," the best government is one "whose principle and foundation is virtue." The only form based upon this principle, Adams argued, is the republican form. Anyone who read the great political philosophers of the seventeenth and eighteenth centuries—Locke, Sidney, Harrington, Burnet, and others—would be convinced "that all good government is republican" and "that the only valuable part of the British constitution is so." A true republic is an "empire of laws," not of men. Therefore, the first question to be asked is "how shall the laws be made?"

They should be made by a representative assembly which should be "an exact portrait, in miniature, of the people at large," said Adams. It should "think, feel, reason and act like them," and thus "great care should be taken . . . to prevent unfair, partial and corrupt elections." Adams favored annual elections, for he believed in the maxim: "Where annual elections end, there slavery begins." The legislative body should be bicameral, for a "*single assembly is liable to all the vices, follies, and frailties of an individual:* subject to fits of humor, transports of passion, partialities of prejudice," avarice, and ambition, "and after some time will vote itself perpetual." A second and distinct house should be created by the elected representatives, either from their own membership or their constituents, or both, and this second assembly, to be called a council, "should be given a free and independent exercise of its judgement upon all acts of legislation, that it may be able to check and arrest the errors of the other." Adams also believed that there should be "a third branch" of legislation, "and wherever the executive power of the state is placed, there the third branch of the legislature ought to be found." The two houses should choose the governor by joint ballot. "*Let him be chosen an-*

Dear Sir

The Subject, on which you was pleased to request my Sentiments, is of infinite Importance to Mankind. Politicks is the Science of human Happiness — and the Felicity of Societies depends entirely on the Constitutions of Government under which they live. —

That famous Couplet of a very great Poet,

    "For Forms of Government let Fools contest

That is best administered, is best," Shews him to have been less attentive to the political and civil Part of History, than the poetical, — He must have read and studied for fanciful Images, not Social Institutions, because the Rectitude of Administration depends upon the Forms; Some Species of Governments being always well administered, others never.

If you can determine, what Form of Government, will produce the greatest Quantity of human Happiness, you will at once decide which is the best, this being the only Criterion. — If you determine what the Dignity of human Nature, and the Happiness of Mankind consists in, you will decide what it is that produces the greatest Quantity of Happiness. — Divines, Novelists, Philosophers, and Men of Pleasure all agree that it consists in Virtue. — If there is a Form of Government, therefore, whose Principle or Foundation is Virtue, will not all those kinds of Men acknowledge, it to be better calculated to promote the general Happiness, than another, the Principle of which is Fear, or even Honour.

I hold the Principle of Honour, Sacred — but am not ashamed to confess myself so much of a Grecian, or Roman, if not of a Christian as to think the Principle of Virtue of higher Rank in the Scale of moral Excellency than Honour. indeed Honour is but a Part, a very Small Part of Virtue. — As to Fear, it is so base and brutal a Passion, that it dont deserve the Name of a Principle, and I think no Gentleman of this Age and Country will think it a Foundation of Government proper for Americans. —

One of the original copies of John Adams's "Thoughts on Government" is held by the North Carolina State Archives. Shown here are the cover page and first page.

nually. Divest him of most of those badges of slavery called prerogatives, and give him a negative on the legislature." The lieutenant governor, secretary, treasurer, and attorney general should also be chosen by joint ballot of both houses. The governor, with the advice and consent of the council, should appoint all judges and justices and all other civil and military officers of the state, "who should have commissions signed by the governor." Sheriffs should be elected by the freeholders of the counties.

The judicial power, according to Adams, should be separate from the legislative and executive powers and independent of both, and the judges should hold office during good behavior. Their salaries should be fixed by law. But something was to be said for the rotation in office of the executive and legislative branches: "A law may be made, that no man shall be governor, lieutenant-governor, secretary, treasurer, counsellor, or representative, more than three years at a time, nor be again elegible until after an interval of three years."

Eventually, when times became more settled, the state might wish to alter the government in such a way as to make it more popular. "Particularly, a plan may be devised . . . *for giving the choice of the governor to the people at large, and of the counsellors to the freeholders of the counties.*" But, whatever the case, two things must be scrupulously observed, Adams concluded: "one is, some regulation for securing forever an equitable choice of representatives; another is, the education of youth, both in literature and morals." [9]

In addition to the county instructions, the Hooper letter, and Adams's "Thoughts on Government," the committee had for its guidance the new constitutions of several states, including those of New Jersey, Delaware, Pennsylvania, Virginia, South Carolina, and Maryland. That these influenced the committee is apparent from the fact that some of the provisions of the North Carolina document were lifted in whole or in part from certain of them, notably those of Virginia and Maryland.[10] It is clear, however, that the most important influences at work in the production of the North Carolina constitution were the English traditions of representative and limited government and, especially, the long experience of developing self-government during the colonial period. The new constitutions of the various states which influenced the North Carolina document, as well as the Adams essay, the Hooper letter, and the county instructions, manifestly reflected those traditions and that experience too.

The document that the committee produced was approved by the congress with little amendment. Thomas Jones gave it its first reading before the house on December 6. On December 9 and 10 it was debated and amended, and on the latter day "ordered to pass for the first reading." Two days later it passed the second reading and the bill of rights was presented to the congress by Thomas Jones. On December 14 the constitution passed its third reading and the bill of rights its first. Both documents received final approval on December 18 when the congress ordered that they be printed and distributed to every county in the state.[11]

The constitution provided for a bicameral legislature, composed of a senate and a house of commons, to be called the General Assembly. Each county, regardless of its population, was to have two representatives and one senator, to be chosen annually by ballot. In addition, the towns of Edenton, New Bern, Wilmington, Salisbury, Hillsborough, and Halifax were to have one representative each. A senator must have lived in the county from which he was chosen for at least a year prior to his election and own at least three hundred acres of land in that county. Representatives must have lived in their counties for at least one year and own one hundred acres of land. The right to vote for senators was granted to all "freemen" twenty-one or more years old who had resided in their county at least one year and had owned a fifty-acre freehold for six months prior to the election. The requirements for voters for members of the commons house were identical except that the property qualification was substantially lower; such voters needed only to have paid public taxes in their county in order to qualify.

Both houses were to be judges of the qualifications of their own members and were granted extensive power. In addition to their legislative powers, they were to appoint jointly all judges of the supreme courts of law and equity, all judges of admiralty, and the attorney general (all of whom were to be commissioned by the governor and hold office during good behavior), all generals and field officers of the state militia and the regular army of the state, the state treasurers, and a secretary. Treasurers were to be appointed annually; the secretary, triannually.

The constitution also gave the General Assembly the power to choose the governor and his council of state, which was to consist of seven members. The governor and council were to be elected annually. The governor, who must have been a resident of the state for five years and the owner of lands and tenements in the state valued at £1,000, could hold office only three years out of every six. The council was charged with the duty of advising "the Governor in the Execution of his Office."

The constitution severely limited the powers of the governor—a natural reaction on the part of the framers to the executive-legislative struggles of the colonial period—and in this respect it was typical of the new constitutions of the other states. It was obviously the objective of the congress to deprive the chief executive of many of the powers that the royal governor had enjoyed, thus making him a weak figure with little or no restraining authority over the legislature. The weakness of executive power was to be a source of consternation and lament to every governor who served during the Revolutionary period as well as a cause of serious inefficiency in government during the remainder of the war years. But it was in the nature of things that the convention should create an executive of this type.

The governor received general executive power and specific grants of authority to "draw for and supply such Sums of Money as shall be voted by the General Assembly for the Contingencies of Government," and, with the advice of his council, power to "lay Embargoes or prohibit the Exportation of any Commodity for any Term not exceeding thirty days . . . in the Recess of the General Assembly." He could also grant pardons and reprieves and, with the advice of the council, fill vacancies temporarily for offices within the appointment of the General Assembly when that body was not in session. The governor was also captain-general and commander-in-chief of the militia and was empowered, when the General Assembly was not in session and with the advice of his council, "to embody the Militia for the public Safety."

But in several important areas the governor had little or no power. He had virtually no power over the patronage. The General Assembly, as we have seen, was to make appointments to the principal judicial posts and other offices of state. Even justices of the county courts were to be recommended by the local representatives in the commons house to the governor, who was to "commission them accordingly." The constitution did not specify the manner in which sheriffs and other county officials were to achieve office, but an ordinance of the convention, passed December 23, provided that sheriffs were to be appointed by the justices of the peace in each county.[12] The constitution also made no provision for an executive veto; and the governor was thus deprived of another important check upon the legislature. Nor did he receive power to convene, prorogue or dissolve the assembly, an important power that the colonial governors had exercised. On the other hand, the assembly had effective checks upon the governor through its power to elect him to office and the general weakness of his constitutional position. The assembly, moreover, had the power to impeach the governor and all other officers of the state for "violating any Part of this Constitution, Mal-Administration or Corruption." The constitution did not provide for the establishment of courts, but it was assumed that the convention and/or the General Assembly would attend to this matter, and this was shortly done.

The constitution reflected greater concern on the part of the congress for separation of powers than for checks and balances. Several provisions prevented persons from holding office in more than one branch of government. Thus, state treasurers, officers of the regular army or navy, supply agents or contractors to the army or navy, judges of the supreme court and the admiralty courts, the secretary of the state, attorney general, and all clerks of courts were prohibited from holding seats in the General Assembly or council of state. Similarly, no member of the council of state could hold a seat in the General Assembly. A further provision stipulated that, "no Person . . . shall hold more than one lucrative Office at any one Time." This provision, however, specifically exempted militia officers and county justices. All persons who had been receivers of public monies were also prohibited from the General Assembly and the council of state until they had "fully accounted for and paid into the Treasury, all sums" for which they were "accountable and liable."

In deference to the large numbers of religious dissenters in the state, in recognition of the extremely weak position of the Anglican church, and doubtless influenced by the general climate of the revolutionary movement in favor of greater freedom in matters of conscience—a climate fostered to a large extent by the humanitarian and skeptical emphasis of the eighteenth-century Enlightenment—the congress wrote into the constitution several provisions designed to bring about and insure separation of church and state. Section XXXIV disestablished the Anglican church: no person would in the future "be compelled to attend any Place of Worship, contrary to his own Faith or Judgement; nor be obliged to pay for the Purchase of any Glebe, or the building of any House of Worship, or for the Maintenance of any Minister or Ministry, contrary to what he believes right, or has voluntarily and personally engaged to perform; but all Persons shall be at Liberty to exercise their own Mode of Worship." A further provision prohibited clergymen of all denominations from holding seats in the General Assembly or council of state.

While the constitution thus severed the ties between church and state and provided for general freedom of worship, it was not completely impartial on the religious issue, for it contained a discriminatory clause against members of non-Protestant sects, thus elevating Protestantism to a position of superiority. This, however, was to be expected, for even amongst the most enlightened of the late eighteenth century Catholicism was regarded with distaste and suspicion, and it was doubtless against Roman Catholics that this clause was directed. It should be noted, however, that the clause applied equally to Jews and Deists. It provided that "no Person who shall deny the being of God, or the Truth of the Protestant Religion, or the Divine Authority either of the Old or New Testament, or who shall hold Religious Principles incompatible with the Freedom and Safety of the State, shall be capable of holding any Office or Place of Trust or Profit in the Civil Department, within this State."

These provisions regarding religion are in no sense remarkable. They were consistent with the general revolutionary trend toward increased religious freedom and disestablishmentarianism. Moreover, dissenting sects had long flourished in North Carolina, while the established church was extremely weak and indeed poverty stricken. Several dissenting sects, including Presbyterians, Methodists, and Baptists, had given strong support to the revolutionary movement, and dissenters had achieved a position of prominence in the provincial congress. Disestablishment was thus a logical result of their support and a guarantee of the continued support of these groups.[13] In actuality, the framers merely wrote into fundamental law the disestablishment of a church that had been established in little more than name for several years. Nevertheless, the provision disestablishing the church was regarded by many as a significant blow struck for greater freedom. John Adams, for example, saw it in this light. "In Virginia and North Carolina," he wrote, "they have made an effort for the destruction of bigotry, which is very remarkable. They have abolished their establishment of Episcopacy so far as to give complete liberty of conscience to dissenters; an acquisition in favor of the rights of mankind, which is worth all the blood and treasure which has been or will be spent in this war." [14]

The disestablishment of the Anglican church in the new states is usually cited as one of the "democratic" advances that resulted from the Revolution, one of the factors, that is, in the advancement of social and economic democracy as distinguished from political democracy. Other features of the North Carolina Constitution of 1776 were designed to obliterate certain practices of the colonial period that worked hardships on certain groups, and thus lessen social and economic inequality. They, too, may be considered as attempts to advance social and economic democracy. Among them was a provision prohibiting imprisonment for debt, except where there was a strong presumption of fraud, after a debtor had delivered up "bona fide, all his Estate, real and personal, for the use of his Creditors. . . ." Another provided that the legislature must in the future "regulate Entails in such a manner as to prevent Perpetuities." A third provided for the establishment of schools "for the convenient Instruction of Youth" at public expense, "and all useful Learning" was to "be duly encouraged and promoted in one or more Universities." These measures undoubtedly received their strongest support from the democratic element in the convention, but they were also measures that the conservatives could accept, if not with enthusiasm, at least without serious concern.

Toward the end of the constitution was a provision incorporating into it the Declaration of Rights, which had been drawn up as a separate document, and warning that the latter "ought never to be violated on any Pretence whatever."[15] The Declaration of Rights was similar to the bills of rights drawn up in the other new states. It was predicated on the assumption that government is the creation of the people and answerable to them for all its actions, and that the individual possesses certain fundamental, unalienable, and inviolable natural rights that it is the duty of government to safeguard. These rights were the heritage of Englishmen and were protected by the common law. The framers wrote these traditional legal guarantees into the Declaration of Rights along with some additional guarantees, the need for which had arisen as a direct result of British practices toward the colonies in the decade before the Revolution. Thus, the document asserted that "all political Power is vested in and derived from the People only" and that the people "ought to have the sole and exclusive Right of regulating the internal Government and Police thereof." Then, after a provision stating that the legislative, executive, and supreme judicial powers "ought to be forever separate and distinct," and another calling for free elections, it listed the fundamental rights that were thereby guaranteed. These included the right of the accused in criminal cases to be informed of the accusation against him, to confront his accusers and witnesses with "other Testimony," to refrain from giving evidence against himself, and to receive a trial by jury. Excessive bails and fines, "cruel and unusual punishment," ex post facto laws, and general search warrants were prohibited. The right of habeas corpus was guaranteed, and no freeman was to be "taken, imprisoned or disseissed of his Freehold, Liberties or Privileges, or outlawed or exiled, or in any Manner destroyed or deprived of his Life, Liberty or Property, but by the Law of the Land." Trial by jury was guaranteed in all cases involving property, as was freedom of the press, assembly, worship, and the right of the people to bear arms. The people were not to be "taxed or made subject to the Payment of any Impost or Duty, without the Consent of themselves or their Representatives in General Assembly freely given." No hereditary emoluments, privileges, or honors were to be granted, and perpetuities and monopolies, which were considered "contrary to the Genius of a free State," were prohibited. The declaration also contained a statement opposing the maintenance of standing armies in time of peace as "dangerous to liberty" and a provision calling for the military to be "kept under strict subordination to, and governed by, the civil Power." [16]

Though basically conservative, the constitution in several respects reflected the wishes of the democratic element at the convention, and to the extent that it did so it was a compromise document. It provided, for example, for popular election of both houses of the legislature, though property requirements were stipulated for voters in both cases and for holders of public office. Eighteenth-century democrats generally championed strong legislatures and weak executives, and such was certainly characteristic of the North Carolina plan. The provisions abolishing imprisonment for debt and entail, those prohibiting plural officeholding, and those providing for public education and the disestablishment of the church were all in harmony with the desires of the democrats. This does not mean, however, that some of these provisions were not favored by conservatives too. John Adams, for example, strongly supported provisions for the public education of youth and religious freedom. Many others who were politically conservative were decidedly liberal in their religious views. Cornelius Harnett, for example, was a Deist, and both Johnston and Hooper opposed the religious test for officeholding that was included in the constitution. Hooper had condemned vigorously a similar provision of the Pennsylvania constitution, and Johnston thought it very unfortunate that the religious test had been introduced at the convention. It was introduced, he reported, by one of the members from the "back Country," had been "carried after a very warm debate," and had "blown up such a flame that every thing" had been in danger of being "thrown into confusion."[17] Both the Orange and Mecklenburg instructions had called for such a test, it will be recalled, and its inclusion thus conformed to the wishes of the dissenting groups of the western and piedmont areas. Many democrats who opposed the Anglican church and worked to bring about its disestablishment were thus in actuality less tolerant in religious matters than others who were politically conservative. At any rate, the provision disestablishing the church conformed to the desires of the democrats, but disestablishment doubtless appealed to many conservatives too. Indeed, it is probable that on several issues of an internal nature democrats and conservatives were not as far apart as they have been represented. Some of the bench marks that are usually labeled democratic gains of the Revolutionary period—in particular, those relating to primogeniture and entail, religion, and the treatment of debtors—were supported, or at least not opposed, by the politically conservative.

Though the constitution contained features that pleased the democratic element, it still provided for a government over which the property-owning middle and upper classes could retain control. In no sense of the word did it create the "simple Democracy" without property qualifications for voting and officeholding that the Mecklenburg instructions had called for. Nor did it provide for the popular election of local justices and other county officials, as the democrats had wished. Moreover, the ban on plural officeholding among officials of the state government did nothing to destroy the old ties between the assembly and the "courthouse rings," for the prohibition did not apply to justices of the peace, and they were still appointed by the governor on the recommendation of the county representatives. Sheriffs, by act of the fifth congress, were to be appointed by the county justices, and local officials were still supported by fees rather than salaries. Thus, the constitution did little to inaugurate more democratic or responsible local government. The "courthouse rings" continued to function, even if deprived of some of their opportunities for corruption. And though the apportionment of representation was a considerable improvement over that which existed in the colonial period when the Albemarle counties had the substantial advantage of five representatives each (as compared to two for the remaining counties), the system of equal representation for each county adopted by the convention still contained inequalities, for the traditionally conservative tidewater counties continued to outweigh the piedmont and west in proportion to population. The Declaration of Rights may have been considered by many democrats a substantial victory for their cause, for it recognized the doctrine of popular supremacy over government in addition to guaranteeing individual rights. But in actuality it did little to advance democracy, for though it set definite limits to the authority of government, in no way did it increase popular participation in government. Finally, the important demand contained in both the Orange and Mecklenburg instructions that the constitution be submitted to the people for their ratification was entirely ignored, and this, as one author has pointed out, "in theory, if not in practice, largely rendered nugatory the distinction between primary and derived power emphasized" by these county instructions.[18]

With the constitution formulated and adopted, the congress took steps to put the new government into effect. It elected Richard Caswell the first governor of the new state and Cornelius Harnett, Thomas Person, William Dry, William Haywood, Edward Starkey, Joseph Leech, and Thomas Eaton members of the council of state. Hooper, Hewes, and Burke were elected delegates to the Continental Congress. The congress also chose admiralty court judges for the ports of Beaufort and Brunswick (Richard Cogdell and Richard Quince) and customs collectors for Currituck, Roanoke, Bath, Beaufort, and Brunswick.[19] It created district criminal courts and appointed two persons in each of the six districts to serve as judges. It also passed an ordinance establishing county courts and appointing justices. The latter were to appoint at their first session "some substantial Freeholder in their County to be Sheriff." The congress further appointed a committee to review all laws then in effect to determine whether or not they were consistent with the new form of government and the situation of the state, to prepare new bills to be passed into law, and to "lay the same before the next General Assembly for their approbation."[20] Finally, it resolved that the first General Assembly under the new constitution should convene at New Bern on April 2, 1777, and provided that the sheriff of each county should hold an election for senators and representatives on March 10. Governor Caswell was directed to assume office as soon as the convention adjourned. It did so December 23.[21]

Thus, the congress completed the transition of North Carolina from colony to state by formulating a system of government that it hoped would serve enduringly the interests of the body politic. There were, of course, many shortcomings in the structure it created. The legislature was too powerful and executive authority too weak. During the remaining years of the Revolution the war governors simply did not have adequate power to deal effectively with the myriad military and economic problems they faced. Equal representation kept the more populous west greatly underrepresented in the legislature, and political power at the state level was thus largely retained by the elite eastern group that had dominated affairs during the royal period. Continued eastern domination was to create serious sectional conflict in the years to come. Local government continued to be undemocratic. A serious deficiency that made basic constitutional revision impossible for the next sixty years was the omission of any provision for amendment. Even so, the new government constituted a distinct advance over that of the royal period. Republican in form and based upon a written constitution that guaranteed fundamental rights and freedoms, it was considerably more liberal than the royal government had been. It was also more liberal than the new governments established by several of the other states. Still, it was only vaguely democratic—at least in the modern sense of that term—but it nevertheless established the foundation upon which greater democracy could build in the nineteenth century. It was, indeed, all that could have been expected given the conditions, traditions, and experience out of which it emerged.

NOTES

Chapter I

1. Evarts B. Greene and Virginia Harrington, *American Population before the Federal Census of 1790* (New York, 1932), 156n, 159, 172; Hugh T. Lefler and Albert R. Newsome, *North Carolina: The History of a Southern State* (Chapel Hill, 1954), 71, hereinafter cited as Lefler and Newsome, *North Carolina.*

2. Lefler and Newsome, *North Carolina,* 71-79; Samuel A. Ashe, *History of North Carolina* (Greensboro, 2 vols., 1908-1925), I, 265-266, 276-279, 319-320, hereinafter cited as Ashe, *History;* William K. Boyd (ed.), *Some Eighteenth Century Tracts Concerning North Carolina* (Raleigh, 1927), 419-420, 424-425, hereinafter cited as Boyd, *North Carolina Tracts.*

3. Paul Conkin, "The Church Establishment in North Carolina, 1765-1776," *North Carolina Historical Review,* XXXII (January, 1955), 7-9; hereinafter this journal will be cited as *NCHR.* Lefler and Newsome, *North Carolina,* 80.

4. Charles Christopher Crittenden, *The Commerce of North Carolina, 1763-1789* (New Haven, 1936), 1, 8, 13, 21-23, 53, 59-60, 63-64, 72-75, 86-88, 94, 96-98.

5. Lefler and Newsome, *North Carolina,* 106-119.

6. Dobbs to Board of Trade, Aug. 3, 1760, William L. Saunders (ed.), *The Colonial Records of North Carolina* (Raleigh, 10 vols., 1886-1890), VI, 279-280, hereinafter cited as Saunders, *Colonial Records.*

7. Charles L. Raper, *North Carolina: A Study in English Colonial Government* (New York, 1904), 33-37, 85, 92-94, 97, hereinafter cited as Raper, *North Carolina Colonial Government;* Florence Cook, "Procedure in the North Carolina Colonial Assembly, 1731-1770," *NCHR,* VIII (July, 1931), 274, 283, hereinafter cited as Cook, "Procedure in Colonial Assembly."

8. Raper, *North Carolina Colonial Government,* 92-93.

9. Raper, *North Carolina Colonial Government,* 94-97.

10. Julian P. Boyd, "The Sheriff in Colonial North Carolina," *NCHR,* V (April, 1928), 172-173, 179-180, hereinafter cited as Boyd, "Sheriff in North Carolina."

11. Lawrence F. London, "The Representation Controversy in Colonial North Carolina," *NCHR,* XI (October, 1934), 255-270.

12. Lefler and Newsome, *North Carolina,* 164.

13. Raper, *North Carolina Colonial Government,* 71-75, 148-163.

14. Raper, *North Carolina Colonial Government,* 148-155. Halifax County was not created until 1758, when it was formed from Edgecombe. The town of Halifax was made its county seat that same year and subsequently the court sat there instead of at Edgecombe Courthouse, which had been designated the court's seat by the act of 1746.

15. Raper, *North Carolina Colonial Government,* 156-163.

16. Boyd, "Sheriff in North Carolina," 151-162. A recent article by Alan D. Watson successfully challenges some of Boyd's conclusions regarding the appointment of sheriffs. For example, Boyd contends that although after 1745 the county courts could nominate any freeholder for sheriff who was not a member of the council or assembly the justices "continued to nominate one another for the office down to the Revolution" (p. 156). He also assumes that the governors invariably appointed the nominees of the county courts. Watson shows that after 1745 "only slightly more than 60 percent of the nominees were justices at the time of their first recommendation." He also shows that in extraordinary cases the governor could make appointments to the office of sheriff independently of the county courts and concludes that more than 10 percent of the sheriffs appointed during the colonial period in the fourteen counties he studied were

not nominees of the courts. See Alan D. Watson, "The Appointment of Sheriffs in Colonial North Carolina: A Reexamination," *NCHR*, LIII (October, 1976), 385-398.

17. Report of Governor Tryon to the Earl of Shelburne, 1767, Saunders, *Colonial Records*, VII, 497.

18. Boyd, "Sheriff in North Carolina," 168-172.

19. Cook, "Procedure in Colonial Assembly," 274; Raper, *North Carolina Colonial Government*, 95.

20. Report of Governor Tryon to the Earl of Shelburne, 1767, Saunders, *Colonial Records*, VII, 497.

21. Raper, *North Carolina Colonial Government*, 145-146, 197-203; Boyd, "Sheriff in North Carolina," 167.

22. Ellis Merton Coulter, "The Granville District," *James Sprunt Historical Publications*, XIII (Chapel Hill, 1913), 32-56.

23. George Sims, "An Address to the People of Granville County," June 6, 1765, Boyd, *North Carolina Tracts*, 186.

24. On the Regulation see Hugh T. Lefler, "Orange County and the War of the Regulation," in Hugh T. Lefler and Paul Wager (eds.), *Orange County—1752-1952* (Chapel Hill, 1953), 24-40; John Spencer Bassett, "The Regulators of North Carolina (1765-1771)," *Annual Report of the American Historical Association for the Year 1894* (Washington, 1895), 141-212; Marvin L. Michael Kay, "The North Carolina Regulation, 1766-1776: A Class Conflict," in Alfred F. Young (ed.), *The American Revolution: Explorations in the History of American Radicalism* (DeKalb, Ill., 1976), 70-123.

Chapter II

1. C. Robert Haywood, "The Mind of the North Carolina Opponents of the Stamp Act," *NCHR*, XXIX (July, 1952), 331-335; Ashe, *History*, I, 315; excerpts from the *North Carolina Gazette*, Nov. 20, 27, 1765; Tryon to Seymore Conway, Dec. 26, 1765, Feb. 25, 1766, Saunders, *Colonial Records*, VII, 123-129, 168c-168f, 143-144, 169-174.

2. Ashe, *History*, I, 335; R. D. W. Connor and others, *History of North Carolina*, Vol. I, *The Colonial and Revolutionary Periods, 1584-1783* (Chicago, 3 vols., 1919), 331-332; Legislative Journals, Dec. 5, 1768, Saunders, *Colonial Records*, VII, 981. The volume by Connor will hereinafter be cited as *Colonial and Revolutionary Periods*.

3. Parliament passed two other Townshend measures relating to colonial affairs in addition to the Revenue Act: an act suspending the New York assembly if it did not comply fully with the terms of the Quartering Act of 1765, and an act establishing a board of commissioners of the customs for the colonies. These measures also produced discontent and protest in the colonies, but the main thrust of colonial opposition was against the Revenue Act.

4. John R. Alden, *The South in the Revolution, 1763-1789* (Baton Rouge, 1957), 109-110; John C. Miller, *Origins of the American Revolution* (Boston, 1948), 269, hereinafter cited respectively as Alden, *South in the Revolution*, and Miller, *Origins of the Revolution*.

5. Legislative Journals, Nov. 2-4, 1769, Tryon to Lord Hillsborough, Nov. 22, 1769, Saunders, *Colonial Records*, VIII, 121-134, 151-152.

6. Tryon to Hillsborough, Feb. 1, 1771, Legislative Journals, Oct. 23, 1769, Saunders, *Colonial Records*, VIII, 495-496, 88-89; Alden, *South in the Revolution*, 115; Miller, *Origins of the Revolution*, 280.

7. Connor, *Colonial and Revolutionary Periods*, 336-337; Alden, *South in the Revolution*, 116.

8. Albert R. Newsome, "Josiah Martin," in Allen Johnson, Dumas Malone, and others (eds.), *Dictionary of American Biography* (New York, 22 vols., 1946), XII, 343.

9. Raper, *North Carolina Colonial Government*, 240; Lefler and Newsome, *North Carolina*, 152.

10. James Hunter to William Butler, Nov. 6, 1772, quoted in Ashe, *History*, I, 404-405.

11. Raper, *North Carolina Colonial Government*, 162, 210-212; Ashe, *History*, I, 408-410.

12. Legislative Journals, Dec. 4, 9, 1773, Saunders, *Colonial Records*, IX, 707-709, 743.

13. Legislative Journals, Dec. 21, 1773, Saunders, *Colonial Records*, IX, 786-788.

14. Charles G. Sellers, Jr., "Making a Revolution: The North Carolina Whigs, 1765-1775," in J. Carlyle Sitterson (ed.), *Studies in Southern History in Memory of Albert Ray Newsome, 1894-1951*, Vol. XXXIX in James Sprunt Studies in History and Political Science (Chapel Hill, 1957), 27-28, hereinafter cited as Sellers, "Making a Revolution."

15. Legislative Journals, March 2, 24, 25, 30, 1774, Saunders, *Colonial Records*, IX, 832-833, 943-944, 950, 954-955.

16. Sellers, "Making a Revolution," 27-28.

17. Mark A. DeWolf Howe (ed.), "Journal of Josiah Quincy, Junior, 1773," Massachusetts Historical Society *Proceedings*, 3d ser. (Boston, 85 vols., 1907-   ), XLIX (1915-1916), 458.

18. Sellers, "Making a Revolution," 29-30.

19. For biographical references to these and other North Carolina revolutionary leaders, consult the bibliographical essay.

20. Johnston to Hooper, April 5, 1774, Saunders, *Colonial Records*, IX, 968.

21. Hamilton J. Eckenrode, *The Revolution in Virginia* (Boston, 1916), 33-34.

22. North Carolina Committee of Correspondence to South Carolina Committee of Correspondence, June 10, 1774, Walter Clark (ed.), *The State Records of North Carolina* (Winston and Goldsboro, 16 vols., 1895-1907), XI, 245-246, hereinafter cited as Clark, *State Records*.

23. Same to Virginia Committee of Correspondence, June 21, 1774, Clark, *State Records*, XI, 247-248.

24. Letter from Wilmington, N.C., to a citizen of Boston, Aug. 2, 1774 (transcript of a letter published in the *Boston Gazette*, Sept. 5, 1774), Miscellaneous Papers, 1755-1788, series I, Vol. I, Archives, North Carolina Division of Archives and History, hereinafter cited as State Archives. North Carolina Committee of Correspondence to Virginia Committee of Correspondence [?], July 28, 1774, Thomas Addison Emmet Collection (transcripts), State Archives.

25. Proceedings of the Wilmington District Meeting, July 21, 1774, Saunders, *Colonial Records*, IX, 1016-1017.

26. Records exist of meetings in the counties of Anson, Rowan, Pitt, Granville, Chowan, and Johnston, and the towns of Halifax and New Bern. Saunders, *Colonial Records*, IX, 1024-1041.

27. Journal of the First Provincial Congress, Aug. 25-27, 1774, Saunders, *Colonial Records*, IX, 1042-1049.

28. Council Journals, Aug. 13, 1774, Proclamation of Governor Martin, Aug. 13, 1774, Martin to Dartmouth, April 6, 1774, Sept. 1, 1774, Martin to a correspondent in England, Nov. 5, 1774, Saunders, *Colonial Records*, IX, 1028-1030, 973-974, 1056, 1087.

29. In some cases committee minutes were not kept or have not been preserved. In more than one instance one finds mention in the sources of the existence of a particular committee yet searches in vain for a record of its minutes. For example, the existence of a committee in Duplin County is mentioned in the proceedings of the Wilmington committee for March 6, 1775, yet no records of this committee at this particular period have been found. For the proceedings of the local committees during this period see Saunders, *Colonial Records*, IX, 1073-1166, passim.

30. The Continental Association was adopted by the Continental Congress on Oct. 18 and signed by the members on Oct. 20, 1774. It provided for the nonimportation and nonconsumption of British goods after Dec. 1, 1774, and for nonexportation to Britain of all goods but rice after Sept. 10, 1775. Other provisions stipulated that slaves were not to be imported after Dec. 1, 1774, that domestic manufactures, agriculture, frugality, economy, and industry were to be encouraged, and that extravagance, dissipation, and expensive diversions and entertainments were to be discouraged. The

First Provincial Congress of North Carolina had already adopted a nonimportation agreement and recommended the appointment of local committees in August, as we have seen, and had committed itself to support the measures of the forthcoming Continental Congress, thus in effect giving advance approval to the Association. The Second Provincial Congress formally approved the Association in April, 1775. Several local versions of the Association circulated in North Carolina during these months. For the text of the Continental Association, see Worthington C. Ford (ed.), *Journals of the Continental Congress, 1774-1789* (Washington, 34 vols., 1904-1937), I, 75-80.

31. Martin to Dartmouth, March 10, 1775, Saunders, *Colonial Records*, IX, 1155.

32. Wilmington Committee to John Hancock, John Rowe, and Samuel Adams, July 29, 1774, John Harvey to James Bowdoin, John Hancock, Samuel Adams, Isaac Smith, and the Boston Committee of Correspondence, Sept. 20, 1774, Miscellaneous Papers, series I, Vol. I, 1755-1788, State Archives; David Jefferies to John Harvey, Oct. 17, 1774, David Jefferies Papers, State Archives; William Hooper to James Iredell, Aug. 5, 1774, Don Higginbotham (ed.), *The Papers of James Iredell* (Raleigh, 2 vols., 1976), I, 244-247, hereinafter cited as Higginbotham, *Iredell Papers*; Proceedings of the New Bern Committee, Jan. 27, 1775, Proceedings of the Pitt County Committee, Feb. 11, 1775, Saunders, *Colonial Records*, IX, 1116, 1126.

33. Letter from a Gentleman at Wilmington, N.C., to a Friend at Boston, Aug. 2, 1774, Peter Force (ed.), *American Archives*, 4th ser. (Washington, 6 vols., 1837-1846), I, 670, hereinafter cited as Force, *American Archives*.

34. Janet Schaw, *Journal of a Lady of Quality*, ed. Evangeline W. Andrews and Charles M. Andrews (New Haven, 1923), 154, hereinafter cited as Schaw, *Journal of a Lady of Quality*.

35. Harvey to the Counties of North Carolina, Feb. 11, 1775, Saunders, *Colonial Records*, IX, 1125.

36. Proclamation of Governor Martin, March 6, 1775, Saunders, *Colonial Records*, IX, 1145-1146.

37. Martin to Dartmouth, April 20, 1775, Saunders, *Colonial Records*, IX, 1228.

38. Proclamation of Governor Martin, April 3, 1775, Journal of the Second Provincial Congress, April 3, 1775, Legislative Journals, April 4, 1775, Martin to Dartmouth April 7, 1775, Saunders, *Colonial Records*, IX, 1177-1178, 1180-1181, 1187-1190, 1212.

39. Martin to Dartmouth, April 7, 1775, Saunders, *Colonial Records*, IX, 1213.

40. Legislative Journals, April 6, 1775, Saunders, *Colonial Records*, IX, 1198-1200.

41. Journal of the Second Provincial Congress, April 5-7, 1775, Saunders, *Colonial Records*, IX, 1180-1185.

42. Legislative Journals, April 7, 1775, Proclamation of Governor Martin, April 8, 1775, Saunders, *Colonial Records*, IX, 1201-1204, 1211.

43. Martin to Dartmouth, April 20, 1775, Legislative Journals, April 7, 1775, Saunders, *Colonial Records*, IX, 1223-1224, 1205.

44. Martin to Dartmouth, April 7, 1775, Saunders, *Colonial Records*, IX, 1214-1215.

Chapter III

1. Martin formulated a plan to mobilize and set in motion toward the east an armed force of backcountry tories in conjunction with a simultaneous British invasion by sea, thereby reestablishing royal control in the province and creating a base from which operations could proceed against the other southern colonies. The plan was approved by the British ministry and put into effect but was completely foiled by the important patriot victory over the tories at Moore's Creek Bridge in February, 1776, discussed later in this chapter. For detailed accounts of these matters see Robert L. Ganyard, "North Carolina during the American Revolution: The First Phase, 1774-1777" (unpublished Ph.D. dissertation, Duke University, 1963), 137-141, 158-159, 240-286, and Hugh F. Rankin, "The Moore's Creek Bridge Campaign," *NCHR*, XXX (January, 1953), 23-60.

2. Martin to Dartmouth, June 30, 1775, Saunders, *Colonial Records*, X, 41-42; Schaw, *Journal of a Lady of Quality*, 186-187.

3. Proceedings of the Committee for the Town of Newbern and County of Craven, May 31, 1775, Hayes MSS, 1775-1779 (photostats), State Archives.

4. Cogdell to Caswell, June 18, 1775, Richard Cogdell Papers, 1774-1789, State Archives; Resolution of the Newbern Committee, June 17, 1775, Hayes Collection Transcripts, 1748-1806, State Archives.

5. Proceedings of the Committee for Newbern and the County of Craven, May 31, 1775, Hayes MSS, 1775-1779 (photostats), State Archives.

6. Resolutions of the Mecklenburg County Committee, May 31, 1775, *North Carolina Gazette*, June 16, 1775.

7. Cogdell to Caswell, June 18, 1775, Cogdell Papers, State Archives; Johnston to Hewes, June 27, 1775, Hayes Collection Transcripts, 1748-1806, State Archives.

8. Proceedings of the Committee for Newbern and the County of Craven, May 31, 1775, Hayes MSS, 1775-1779 (photostats), State Archives.

9. Schaw, *Journal of a Lady of Quality*, 199-200.

10. Proceedings of the Pitt County Committee, July 1, 8, 1775, John Simpson to Cogdell, July 15, 1775, Saunders, *Colonial Records*, X, 62-64, 87, 94-95.

11. Martin's denial was made in a letter to Louis Henry DeRosset, a wealthy loyalist and council member. This letter fell into the hands of the New Bern committee, which rejected completely the governor's claim that he was not involved. Proceedings of the Newbern Committee, Aug. 2, 1775, Saunders, *Colonial Records*, X, 138a.

12. Cogdell to Caswell, June 18, 1775, Cogdell Papers, State Archives; John Drayton, *Memoirs of the American Revolution* (Charleston, 2 vols., 1821), I, 309-310, 344-346; Martin to Dartmouth, July 6, 1775, North Carolina Delegates in the Continental Congress to the Provincial Congress of New York, July 8, 1775, Saunders, *Colonial Records*, X, 69-70, 84; Committee of Intelligence of Charleston to the Newbern Committee, July 4, 1775, Force, *American Archives*, 4th series, II, 1568.

13. On Indian affairs at this time consult Robert L. Ganyard, "Threat from the West: North Carolina and the Cherokee, 1776-1778," *NCHR*, XLV (January, 1968), 47-66, and James H. O'Donnell III, *Southern Indians in the American Revolution* (Knoxville, Tenn., 1973), 28-53.

14. Typical was the work of Samuel Johnston. See his letter to Hewes, June 11, 1775, Hayes Collection Transcripts, 1748-1806, State Archives.

15. The letter received widespread and rapid circulation. It was published in the *North Carolina Gazette* on July 7. By that date copies had already been received in Mecklenburg and Orange counties in the west. Salem Diary, July 7, 1775, Adelaide Lisetta Fries and others (eds.), *Records of the Moravians in North Carolina* (Raleigh, 11 vols., 1922-1969), II, 876, hereinafter cited as Fries, *Moravian Records*; North Carolina Delegates in the Continental Congress to the People of North Carolina, June 19, 1775, Hayes Collection Transcripts, 1748-1806, State Archives.

16. Ganyard, "North Carolina during the American Revolution," 163-178. The author has been able to find no evidence of the organization of committees by the end of August, 1775, only in the following counties: Chatham, Johnston, Edgecombe, Tyrrell, and Hyde. Of these five, Chatham, Johnston, and Edgecombe were located in the piedmont, where tory sentiment was strong. Tyrrell and Hyde were contiguous, rather isolated, and sparsely populated counties on the coast. They formed a peninsula bounded by Albemarle and Pamlico sounds. Lack of evidence, of course, does not mean that committees were not formed in these five counties.

17. Bagge MSS, 1776, Fries, *Moravian Records*, III, 1024.

18. Force, *American Archives*, 4th series, III, 40; Proceedings of the Rowan County Committee, Sept. 21, Oct. 17, Nov. 10, 1775, Proceedings of the Newbern Committee, July 21, Aug. 5, 1775, Martin to Dartmouth, June 30, 1775, Saunders, *Colonial Records*, X, 253-254, 280, 316-317, 115-116, 139, 48; Force, *American Archives*, 4th series, III, 100.

19. Proceedings of the Wilmington Committee, Aug. 18, 19, 1775, Saunders, *Colonial Records*, X, 160-161; Robert Smith to _____, May 23, 1775, Mrs. Cullen Pollok to Hewes, Dec. 23, 1775, Hayes Collection, film, reel 3, Southern Historical Collection,

University of North Carolina at Chapel Hill; Johnston to Hewes, Nov. 26, 1775, enclosed in a letter from Vice-Admiral Graves to Philip Stevens, Jan. 29, 1776, English Records, Colonial Office Papers (transcripts), State Archives; *North Carolina Gazette*, Dec. 22, 1775; Hooper to James Iredell, Jan. 6, 1776, Higginbotham, *Iredell Papers*, I, 339-340.

20. Robert Nelson to Henry Nelson, Oct. 20, 1775, English Records, Colonial Office Papers (transcripts), State Archives; Bagge MSS, 1776, Fries, *Moravian Records*, II, 850; John Dunn to _____, 1776, same to Samuel Ashe, Sept. 11, 1776, Clark, *State Records*, XIX, 898-903; XV, 691; South Carolina Committee of Intelligence to Wilmington Committee, June 6, 1775, Hayes MSS, 1775-1779 (photostats), State Archives.

21. Bishop Graff to the United Elders Conference, Sept. 30, 1775, Salem Diary, Aug. 28, 1775, Bethabara Diary, Aug. 28, 1776, Fries, *Moravian Records*, II, 885, 882, 904-905; Proceedings of the Bute County Committee, Nov. 14, 1775, Thomas M. Pittman Collection, Bute County Records, 1771-1779, State Archives; Proceedings of the Tryon County Committee, Oct. 25, 1775, Jan., 1776, Proceedings of the Pitt County Committee, April 23, Feb. 13, 1776, Proceedings of the Newbern District Committee, Feb. 23, 1776, Proceedings of the Newbern Committee, Feb. 21, 24, 1776, Proceedings of the Rowan County Committee, Aug. 1, Nov. 8, 1775, Feb. 7, 1776, Saunders, *Colonial Records*, X, 297, 424, 499, 451, 462, 459-461, 137, 310, 433.

22. Proceedings of the Third Provincial Congress, Aug. 20-23, Sept. 8, 1775, Saunders, *Colonial Records*, X, 164-169, 173-174, 201-203; Bagge MSS, 1776, Fries, *Moravian Records*, II, 849; Johnston to Iredell, Aug. 22, 1775, Charles E. Johnson Collection, State Archives. The Moravians, who were settled in Surry County, were fairly recent arrivals from Pennsylvania. A devoutly religious group, they had scruples against bearing arms, had no firm convictions about the revolutionary conflict, and sought to remain neutral. The Scots Highlanders, also for the most part recent arrivals, had little or no sentimental attachment to America and its institutions and little understanding of the controversy with Britain. They had been allowed to migrate to Carolina and settle on crown lands, and they had taken a solemn oath of loyalty to the crown. Their leaders, some of whom had left behind estates in Scotland which might be confiscated if they supported the American rebellion and some of whom were army officers on half pay, were generally ardent champions of the royal cause. The common people were intensely loyal to their leaders and naturally followed them. The Highlanders were North Carolina's most zealous loyalists. See Ian Charles Cargill Graham, *Colonists from Scotland: Emigration to North America, 1707-1783* (Ithaca, 1956), 150-151, 154, and Robert O. DeMond, *The Loyalists of North Carolina during the Revolution* (Durham, 1940), 51-52.

23. Journal of the Third Provincial Congress, Aug. 22-25, 28, 1775, Saunders, *Colonial Records*, X, 170-172, 181-182.

24. Under the terms of a former superior court law the colony had been divided into six judicial districts. These were now utilized for political and military purposes. The six districts were named after the principal towns in each: Wilmington, New Bern, Edenton, Halifax, Hillsborough, and Salisbury. Journal of the Third Provincial Congress, Aug. 31, Sept. 1, 8, 9, 1775, Saunders, *Colonial Records*, X, 185-187, 203-207.

25. Journal of the Third Provincial Congress, Sept. 7, 10, 1775, Saunders, *Colonial Records*, X, 194-200, 216-219. The provincial congress sometimes issued currency in dollar denominations, sometimes in pounds. Sometimes currency would be issued in dollar denominations, but the amount of bounties or invoices would be designated in pounds, shillings and pence, and vice versa. The conversion rate was two and a half to one; that is, two and one-half dollars equalled one pound. There were eight shillings in a provincial dollar, twenty in a pound.

26. The stated reason for the concession, however, was that many "substantial Inhabitants" who ought to have the right to vote lived in these counties but had been unable to secure freehold title to the land they occupied because these counties were located in the Granville District. Journal of the Third Provincial Congress, Aug. 24,

96

Sept. 9, 1775, Saunders, *Colonial Records*, X, 175, 208-214.

27. Journal of the Provincial Council, Oct. 18, 1775, Martin to Dartmouth, Oct. 16, 1775, Saunders, *Colonial Records*, X, 175, 283, 269.

28. Journal of the Provincial Council, Oct. 18-22, Dec. 18-24, 1775, Feb. 28-March 5, 1776, Saunders, *Colonial Records*, X, 283-294, 349-362, 469-477; Christopher Ward, *The War of the Revolution*, ed. John R. Alden (New York, 2 vols., 1952), II, 845-849; David Duncan Wallace, *South Carolina: A Short History, 1520-1948* (Chapel Hill, 1951), 264.

29. Ganyard, "North Carolina during the American Revolution," 240-286; Rankin, "Moore's Creek Bridge Campaign," 23-60.

30. Journal of the Fourth Provincial Congress, April 4-May 14, 1776, correspondence between the inhabitants of Wilmington and the British authorities, Feb. 27, 1776, Saunders, *Colonial Records*, X, 499-571, passim, 477-481; extract of a letter written by an officer of the Fifteenth British Regiment, May 17, 1776, Clark, *State Records*, XI, 297-298; James Moore to Charles Lee, May 19, 1776, *The Lee Papers* (New York, 4 vols., 1872-1875, in *Collections of the New York Historical Society*), II, 28.

31. Journal of the Fourth Provincial Congress, April 5, 8, 9, 15, 16, 1776, Saunders, *Colonial Records*, X, 502, 504, 506-507, 516, 519.

32. Journal of the Fourth Provincial Congress, April 10, 13, 15, 20, 29, May 3, 9, 10, 11, 1776, Saunders, *Colonial Records*, X, 508, 513-514, 516-517, 528, 546, 558, 575, 577; Hewes to Johnston, May 16, 1776, Clark, *State Records*, XXII, 517.

33. Journal of the Fourth Provincial Congress, May 4, 1776, Saunders, *Colonial Records*, X, 560-563.

34. Journal of the Fourth Provincial Congress, April 19, 24, May 6, 1776, Saunders, *Colonial Records*, X, 524-526, 537-540, 565, 572-573.

35. The change in attitude is revealed in the following documents: James Iredell, "Causes Leading up to the American Revolution" (June, 1776), James Iredell MSS, Princeton University Library, on film at the Southern Historical Collection, Chapel Hill. Hewes to Johnston, Dec. 1, 1775, Edmund Cody Burnett (ed.), *Letters of Members of the Continental Congress* (Washington, 8 vols., 1921-1936), I, 266-267; same to same, March 20, 1776, Clark, *State Records*, XI, 288-289; Hooper to Iredell, Jan. 6, 1776, Higginbotham, *Iredell Papers*, I, 339-340; same to Johnston, Feb. 6, 1776, Thomas Addison Emmet Collection, 1757-1847, State Archives; Johnston to Hewes, March 3, April 4, 15, 1776, Hooper to Hewes, April 17, 1776, Hayes Collection Transcripts, 1748-1806, State Archives; Hewes to Johnston, Feb. 13, 1776, John Penn to Thomas Person, Feb. 14, 1776, Burnett, *Letters of Congress*, I, 344, 349; Johnston to Iredell, April 5, 1776, Saunders, *Colonial Records*, X, 1032; Penn to John Adams, April 17, 1776, Force, *American Archives*, 4th series, V, 959. This letter is identified in Force only as a letter from "a gentleman in North Carolina." It is identified as a letter from Penn to Adams in R. D. W. Connor, *Cornelius Harnett: An Essay in North Carolina History* (Raleigh, 1909), 140.

36. Journal of the Third Provincial Congress, Sept. 4, 1775, Saunders, *Colonial Records*, X, 192.

37. Journal of the Fourth Provincial Congress, April 12, 1776, Saunders, *Colonial Records*, X, 512.

38. The committee was composed of Samuel Johnston, Abner Nash, Cornelius Harnett, Thomas Jones, Green Hill, Thomas Burke, Allen Jones, Matthew Locke, Jacob Blount, John Rand, John Johnston, Samuel Ashe, John Kinchen, Samuel Spencer, William Haywood, Nathaniel Richardson, John Bradford, Ambrose Ramsey, Thomas Person, William Hooper, and John Penn. Journal of the Fourth Provincial Congress, April 13, 15, 1776, Saunders, *Colonial Records*, X, 515-516.

39. On Thomas Burke, consult Elisha Douglass, "Thomas Burke: Disillusioned Democrat," *NCHR*, XXVI (April, 1949), 150-186; on Thomas Person, J. G. de Roulhac Hamilton's essay in *Dictionary of American Biography*, XIV, 496.

40. Johnston to Iredell, April 20, 1776, Saunders, *Colonial Records*, X, 498-499.

41. Journal of the Fourth Provincial Congress, April 27, 1776, Thomas Jones to Iredell, April 28, 1776, Saunders, *Colonial Records*, X, 545, 1033-1034.

42. Journal of the Fourth Provincial Congress, April 30, 1776, Saunders, *Colonial Records*, X, 552.

43. Journal of the Fourth Provincial Congress, May 11, 1, 14, 1776, Saunders, *Colonial Records*, X, 579-582, 553, 589.

44. Journal of the Council of Safety, June 5-July 16, July 21-Aug. 28, Sept. 6-13, Sept. 27-Oct. 25, 1776, Saunders, *Colonial Records*, X, 618d-647, 682-707, 826-830, 873-881.

45. Ganyard, "Threat from the West," 47-66; O'Donnell, *Southern Indians*, 28-53.

46. Petition of the Watuga [*sic*] Settlers, Aug., 1776, Journal of the Council of Safety, Aug. 22, 1776, Journal of the Fifth Provincial Congress, Nov. 19, 1776, Saunders, *Colonial Records*, X, 708-711, 702, 926.

Chapter IV

1. Journal of the Council of Safety, Aug. 9, 1776, Saunders, *Colonial Records*, X, 696.

2. For a detailed discussion and analysis of these elections see Robert L. Ganyard, "Radicals and Conservatives in Revolutionary North Carolina: A Point at Issue, the October Election, 1776," *William and Mary Quarterly*, 3d ser., XXIV (October, 1967), 568-587.

3. Journal of the Fifth Provincial Congress, Nov. 12, 13, 14, 15, 18, 1776, Saunders, *Colonial Records*, X, 913, 916-919, 921, 924. Sixteen members represented eastern counties; twelve piedmont or western counties. These figures are based upon a division of the state into its seventeen easternmost and eighteen westernmost counties. The line of division runs along the eastern boundaries of Northampton, Halifax, Edgecombe, Johnston, Duplin and Bladen counties.

4. Journal of the Fifth Provincial Congress, Dec. 10, 1776, Saunders, *Colonial Records*, X, 963.

5. Hooper to the Fifth Provincial Congress, Oct. 26, 1776, Saunders, *Colonial Records*, X, 862-870.

6. Instructions to the delegates of Orange and Mecklenburg counties, 1776, Saunders, *Colonial Records*, X, 870a-870h.

7. Hooper to the Fifth Provincial Congress, Oct. 26, 1776, Saunders, *Colonial Records*, X, 866-869; see also Hooper to "My Dear Friends," Oct. 27, 1776, Hayes Collection Transcripts, 1748-1806, State Archives. For interesting articles on the application of the theory of mixed government to the British constitution see Corinne Comstock Weston, "Beginnings of the Classical Theory of the English Constitution," *Proceedings of the American Philosophical Society*, C, no. 2 (April, 1956), 133-144, and "The Theory of Mixed Monarchy Under Charles I and After," *English Historical Review*, LXXV (July, 1960), 426-443. The Delaware, New Jersey, and South Carolina constitutions were all conservative documents providing for bicameral legislatures, high property qualifications for the franchise, and very high property qualifications for office. None of them was submitted to the people for ratification.

8. See John Adams to James Warren, April 20, 1776, *Adams-Warren Letters*, Massachusetts Historical Society *Collections*, Vol. LXXII (Boston, 2 vols., 1917-1925), I, 230-231; and Charles F. Adams (ed.), *The Works of John Adams* (Boston, 10 vols., 1850-1856), I, 208-209, hereinafter cited as Adams, *Works of John Adams*.

9. Adams to John Penn, April, 1776. This letter, which was also sent to William Hooper, is included together with the pamphlet version entitled, "Thoughts on Government: Applicable to the Present State of the American Colonies. In a Letter from a Gentleman to his Friend," in Adams, *Works of John Adams*, IV, 193-208. A similar letter was sent by Adams to Thomas Burke and may be found in the Thomas Burke Letterbook, 1774-1781, State Archives. This copy is published in Clark, *State Records*, XI, 321-327.

10. For a detailed analysis of the manner in which other state constitutions were utilized in the drafting of the North Carolina document consult Earle H. Ketcham, "The Sources of the North Carolina Constitution of 1776," *NCHR*, VI (July, 1929), 215-236.

11. Journal of the Fifth Provincial Congress, Dec. 6, 9-10, 12, 14, 18, Saunders, *Colonial Records*, X, 954, 962-963, 967, 969, 974.

12. Ordinance of the Fifth Provincial Congress, Dec. 23, 1776, Clark, *State Records*, XXIII, 992-996.

13. An interesting letter from Thomas Jones to Joseph Hewes, June 28, 1775, records the support of the Methodist and Baptist clergy: "The 20th July the day set apart by the [Continental] Congress for fasting & praying will be observed here and we shall give notice to the people of all denominations for the same purpose . . . we have secured the Preachers and heads of the Methodist & Annabaptists Ch in favour of the Common cause. They preach up resistance . . . to Taxes Popery and Arbitrary power the K＿g and parliament are in pursuit of. . . . Dr. Dove declared from his pulpit to a very large Congregation that he knew of his own certain knowledge Lord North was a second Cousin of the present pope and the whole of them believed it." Hayes MSS, 1775-1779 (photostats), State Archives. Not all dissenters, of course, supported the Revolution. The Quakers and Moravians both sought to remain neutral. Those Presbyterians who were also Scots Highlanders were for the most part loyalists. And at least two Baptist preachers had loyalist sympathies. James Terry and James Childs, both of Anson County, were denounced as loyalists. Terry was sent before the fifth congress charged with preaching "pernicious" political doctrine to the people of the county, and with considerable success, "especially with those of his own Profession." Childs was condemned as an "Enemy of this State" by the council of safety and confined to the town of Edenton. Samuel Spencer to Caswell, Nov. 6, 1776, Secretary of State Papers, 1776, State Archives; Journal of the Council of Safety, Aug. 13, 1776, Saunders, *Colonial Records*, X, 699-700.

14. John Adams to James Warren, Feb. 3, 1777, Adams, *Works of John Adams*, IX, 451.

15. The constitution may be found in Saunders, *Colonial Records*, X, 1006-1013.

16. Declaration of Rights, 1776, Clark, *State Records*, XXIII, 977-979.

17. Hooper to Johnston, Sept. 26, 1776, Saunders, *Colonial Records*, X, 819-820; Johnston to Hannah Iredell, Dec. 13, 1776, Charles E. Johnson Collection, 1755-1779, State Archives.

18. Elisha P. Douglass, *Rebels and Democrats: The Struggle for Equal Political Rights and Majority Rule during the American Revolution* (Chapel Hill, 1955), 132. For the analysis of the conservative nature of the constitution in the foregoing paragraph the author has drawn to a considerable extent upon the excellent discussion in the work cited, pp. 131-135.

19. Ordinance of the Fifth Provincial Congress, Dec. 20, 1776, Clark, *State Records*, XXIII, 986; Journal of the Fifth Provincial Congress, Dec. 20, 22, 23, 1776, Saunders, *Colonial Records*, X, 977, 998, 981.

20. Ordinance of the Fifth Provincial Congress, Dec. 21, 23, 1776, Clark, *State Records*, XXIII, 987, 990, 992-996. The men appointed to this committee were Samuel Johnston, though he was not a delegate to the congress, Thomas Jones, Archibald Maclaine, James Iredell, Abner Nash, Christopher Neale, Samuel Ashe, Waightstill Avery, Samuel Spencer, Jasper Charlton, and John Penn.

21. Journal of the Fifth Provincial Congress, Dec. 20, 23, 1776, Saunders, *Colonial Records*, X, 979, 1001, 1003; Ordinance of the Fifth Provincial Congress, Dec. 20, 1776, Clark, *State Records*, XXIII, 986.

Bibliographical Essay

Several manuscript collections provide valuable insights into politics and government in Revolutionary North Carolina. Among the most important are the Hayes Collection Transcripts, 1748-1806, the Hayes MSS, 1775-1779 (photostats), the Richard Cogdell Papers, 1774-1789, the Charles E. Johnson Collection, 1755-1779, the Thomas Burke Letterbook, 1774-1781, and the Thomas Addison Emmet Collection, 1757-1847 (transcripts of papers in the New York Public Library), all at the State Archives, Raleigh, and the Thomas Burke Papers, 1744-1789, at the Southern Historical Collection, Chapel Hill.

Among the published primary sources, indispensable are William L. Saunders (ed.), *The Colonial Records of North Carolina* (Raleigh, 10 vols., 1886-1890), and Walter Clark (ed.), *The State Records of North Carolina* (Winston and Goldsboro, 16 vols., 1895-1907). Extremely useful, especially for events in the west, is Adelaide L. Fries and others (eds.), *The Records of the Moravians in North Carolina* (Raleigh, 11 vols., 1922-1969). Many pertinent documents may also be found in Peter Force (ed.), *American Archives*, 4th and 5th series, (Washington, 9 vols., 1837-1853), in Edmund C. Burnett (ed.), *Letters of Members of the Continental Congress* (Washington, 8 vols., 1921-1936), and in Don Higginbotham (ed.), *The Papers of James Iredell* (Raleigh, 2 vols., 1976).

Standard histories of North Carolina which devote attention to the period covered by this study are Hugh T. Lefler and Albert R. Newsome, *North Carolina: The History of a Southern State* (Chapel Hill, 1954), Hugh T. Lefler and William S. Powell, *Colonial North Carolina: A History* (New York, 1973), Robert D. W. Connor, *History of North Carolina: The Colonial and Revolutionary Periods, 1584-1783* (Chicago, 1919), and Samuel A. Ashe, *History of North Carolina* (Greensboro, 2 vols., 1908-1925). The last named work has stood the test of time extremely well. To view events in North Carolina in the perspective of revolutionary developments in the other southern colonies consult John R. Alden, *The South in the Revolution, 1763-1789* (Baton Rouge, 1957).

The most detailed and comprehensive account of the Revolution in North Carolina for the period on which this study concentrates, 1774-1776, is Robert L. Ganyard, "North Carolina during the American

Revolution: The First Phase, 1774-1777" (unpublished Ph.D. dissertation, Duke University, 1963). An older study that treats the same period is Enoch W. Sikes, *The Transition of North Carolina from Colony to Commonwealth*, in the Johns Hopkins University Studies in Historical and Political Science, XVI (1898), 475-561. The origins of North Carolina's revolutionary movement are ably treated in Lindley S. Butler, "The Coming of the Revolution in North Carolina" (unpublished Ph.D. dissertation, University of North Carolina, 1971) and his briefer *North Carolina and the Coming of the Revolution, 1763-1776* (Raleigh, 1976). The standard institutional account of government in colonial North Carolina is Charles L. Raper, *North Carolina: A Study in English Colonial Government* (New York, 1904), but it should be supplemented with Jack P. Greene, *The Quest for Power: The Lower Houses of Assembly in the Southern Royal Colonies, 1689-1776* (Chapel Hill, 1963), and the articles by Julian P. Boyd, Florence Cook, Lawrence F. London, and Ellis M. Coulter cited in the notes to chapter one. Especially good on the relationship of the court controversy to the developing Revolution in North Carolina are Charles Grier Sellers, Jr., "Making a Revolution: The North Carolina Whigs, 1765-1775," in J. Carlyle Sitterson (ed.), *Studies in Southern History in Memory of Albert Ray Newsome, 1894-1951*, Vol. XXXIX of the James Sprunt Studies in History and Political Science (Chapel Hill, 1957), 23-46, and H. Braughn Taylor, "The Foreign Attachment Law and the Coming of the Revolution in North Carolina," *North Carolina Historical Review*, LII (January, 1975), 20-36. On the regulator movement consult the works cited in the notes to chapter one. The standard account of the Stamp Act controversy in the colonies is Edmund S. and Helen M. Morgan, *The Stamp Act Crisis: Prologue to Revolution* (Chapel Hill, 1953). For the details of the controversy in North Carolina see Robert C. Haywood, "The Mind of the North Carolina Opponents of the Stamp Act," *North Carolina Historical Review*, VI (July, 1952), 317-343, and Butler, "Coming of the Revolution in North Carolina."

North Carolina's loyalists are given detailed though not definitive treatment in Robert O. DeMond, *The Loyalists of North Carolina during the Revolution* (Durham, 1940) and Carole W. Troxler, *The Loyalist Experience in North Carolina* (Raleigh, 1976). The loyalist uprising of 1776 is ably dealt with in Hugh F. Rankin, "The Moore's Creek Bridge Campaign," *North Carolina Historical Review*, XXX (January, 1953), 23-60. For the Indian campaign of 1776 and the role played therein by the council of safety see Robert L. Ganyard, "Threat from the West: North Carolina and the Cherokee, 1776-1778,"

North Carolina Historical Review, XLV (January, 1968), 47-66. On the state Constitution of 1776 and the character of state politics in the several months before its adoption consult Elisha P. Douglass, *Rebels and Democrats: The Struggle for Equal Political Rights and Majority Rule during the American Revolution* (Chapel Hill, 1955); Fletcher M. Green, *Constitutional Development in the South Atlantic States, 1776-1860: A Study in the Evolution of Democracy* (Chapel Hill, 1930); Earle H. Ketcham, "The Sources of the North Carolina Constitution of 1776," *North Carolina Historical Review*, VI (July, 1929), 215-236; Frank Nash, "The North Carolina Constitution of 1776 and Its Makers," *James Sprunt Studies in History and Political Science*, XI (1912), 7-23; and Robert L. Ganyard, "Radicals and Conservatives in Revolutionary North Carolina: A Point at Issue, the October Election, 1776," *William and Mary Quarterly*, 3d ser., XXIV (October, 1967), 568-587.

Certain leaders have been given more extended treatment in the following: C. B. Alexander, "The Training of Richard Caswell," and "Richard Caswell, Versatile Leader of the Revolution," *North Carolina Historical Review*, XXIII (January, April, 1946), 13-31, 119-141; R. D. W. Connor, "Governor Samuel Johnston of North Carolina," *North Carolina Booklet*, XI (April, 1912), 259-285, and *Cornelius Harnett: An Essay in North Carolina History* (Raleigh, 1909); Elisha P. Douglass, "Thomas Burke: Disillusioned Democrat," *North Carolina Historical Review*, XXVI (April, 1949), 150-186; Blackwell P. Robinson, "Willie Jones of Halifax," *North Carolina Historical Review*, XVIII (January, April, 1941), 1-26, 133-170; R. D. W. Connor, "John Harvey," *North Carolina Booklet*, VIII (July, 1908), 3-42; and Walter Sikes, "Joseph Hewes," *North Carolina Booklet*, IV (September, 1904), 25-36. An able study of William Tryon is Alonzo T. Dill, *Governor Tryon and His Palace* (Chapel Hill, 1955). A recently published account of the role of North Carolina's delegates in the Continental Congress is David T. Morgan and William J. Schmidt, *North Carolinians in the Continental Congress* (Winston-Salem, 1976). Finally, two recent articles on Josiah Martin shed new light on his background and character: Vernon O. Stumpf, "Josiah Martin and His Search for Success: The Road to North Carolina," *North Carolina Historical Review*, LIII (January, 1976), 55-79; and Richard B. Sheridan, "The West Indian Antecedents of Josiah Martin, Last Royal Governor of North Carolina," *North Carolina Historical Review*, LIV (July, 1977), 253-270.

About the Author

A native of Ohio, Robert L. Ganyard received B.A. and M.A. degrees from the University of Buffalo, now the State University of New York at Buffalo, and his Ph.D. from Duke University. He has taught at the University of Houston and the University of Tennessee, Knoxville, and he is currently associate professor of history and director of Interdisciplinary Degree Programs in the Social Sciences at the State University of New York, Buffalo. A specialist in early American history, he has published articles and reviews in leading historical journals and is at work on a comprehensive history of North Carolina in the American Revolution. Married, with three children, he makes his home in Lockport, New York.